D0045893

THE SACRED 6

THE SACRED

6

The Simple Step-by-Step Process for Focusing
Your Attention & Recovering Your Dreams

JB GLOSSINGER

HAY
HOUSE

HAY HOUSE, INC.
Carlsbad, California • New York City
London • Sydney • Johannesburg
Vancouver • Hong Kong • New Delhi

Published and distributed in the United States by: Hay House, Inc.: www.hayhouse.com® • *Published and distributed in Australia by:* Hay House Australia Pty. Ltd.: www.hayhouse.com.au • *Published and distributed in the United Kingdom by:* Hay House UK, Ltd.: www.hayhouse.co.uk • *Published and distributed in the Republic of South Africa by:* Hay House SA (Pty), Ltd.: info@hayhouse.co.za • *Distributed in Canada by:* Raincoast Books: www.raincoast.com • *Published in India by:* Hay House Publishers India: www.hayhouse.co.in

Cover design: Nita Ybarra • *Cover Jacket and Interior design:* Bryn Starr Best

Library of Congress Cataloging-in-Publication Data is on file with the Library of Congress

Hardcover ISBN: 978-1-4019-4798-9
10 9 8 7 6 5 4 3 2 1
1st edition, May 2016

Printed in the United States of America

*To Mom, for always believing in me,
whatever I was doing.*

*To Pilar, for hanging in through it all and being
the rock I could always count on.*

*To my boys—Shadow, Phi Phi, Bud, Raider,
Kaos, Niko, and Neo—and all the other animals
who have been such a wonderful part of my life,
for bringing me your wagging tails
and energy every day.*

CONTENTS

INTRODUCTION

I walk up the worn-out, creaking staircase to the second floor of the library, Dewey decimal numbers firmly in hand. I am on the hunt for a hallowed text—a book that will show me the path to the hidden treasure within myself. Finding my way through the stacks, I stop in front of a tattered leather-bound volume. Sliding it off the shelf, I sit down in the aisle and begin to turn the pages, just as I have done so many times before. A deathlike silence surrounds me, but my inner world is all abuzz. The answers are right there on the page, the secrets to manifesting the life of my dreams, from keeping the right mind-set to understanding the process. I can feel the energy of the words start to surge through me. What a joy to experience! What magic! I have unlocked another piece of the puzzle of living a life of freedom, happiness, and peace.

As a kid I always wanted to be an archeologist. I dreamed of discovering fantastic treasures, hidden secrets, and esoteric wisdom. Growing up blue-collar in northern Indiana, I thought archeological adventure was something I could only read about in books. And read I did. I spent years in libraries, researching human potential, performance, and happiness.

In the process, and much to my surprise, I *did* become an archeologist—an archeologist of life.

Over the past 40-odd years, my search through ancient and modern teachings has taken me on an amazing journey. The more pieces of the mystery I've uncovered, the better my life has become. For a long time I didn't openly discuss my findings with friends or family, for I felt that if I did, those ideas might lose some of their magic. I wanted to prove that they worked before I revealed them, and truth be told, at the time I didn't have much faith in my ability to make them work. As with most experimental research, not everything went according to plan. But just as a master alchemist has to work with lead in order to make gold, the bad and the good contributed equally to my transformation—a transformation that took me from working 60 disorganized hours a week just to survive to a life of fulfillment and productivity in which it takes me 60 *minutes or less* to do the same amount of work as before!

I am now ready to share the results of my years of personal transformation research. The process I have discovered will maximize your focus and productivity while banishing feelings of hopelessness and a sense of being overwhelmed. It can bring success in all areas of your life, transform your relationship with yourself and others, provide for a full expression of your values, and help you build a lasting legacy that will benefit the world around you. I call this process *the Sacred Six.*

WHY SACRED? WHY SIX?

I used to write goals and to-do lists by the thousands, yet I would achieve hardly anything. I struggled with focusing my attention on building the life of my dreams, until I finally discovered the holdback: I was not setting the right goals or taking the steps to achieve them. That is what I am going to help you overcome in this book— misaligned goals and to-do lists that get you nowhere. The goals you will be setting are so important in creating a clear path to the life you desire that you will hold them sacred.

Sacred is a word dear to my heart. When something is sacred, it is not just important; its meaning goes deeper than that. The Sacred Six process will bring you to the full expression of your life purpose, and you can't get any more sacred than that.

Six is more practical. On average, most people can focus on only so many items at once. Six is the ideal number—the sweet spot, if you will—in most areas of the Sacred Six process, including how many daily activities you can effectively handle. Six is also the magic number in managing your time. For instance, let's say you work a standard eight-hour day. If we analyze your productivity, you will probably find that you are putting in only about six hours of *truly* quality work per day.

You're likely to be working on many projects and activities at once—anything from starting a business to improving your golf game to learning a new language. In my years of coaching thousands of people, I have found that six projects at a time is the tipping point—working on any more than that will yield diminishing returns. Feeling overwhelmed, you are unlikely to get any of them done.

On the flip side, maybe you have a few big dreams and a manageable number of goals in mind, but you haven't taken the first step toward charting out how to realize them. The Sacred Six process will help you create an effective action plan and map the way to reach your goals.

So six is the key number. The Sacred Six is a transformational process that helps you narrow your focus to the six projects you will be working on at any given time. Anything that is not on that list, you don't do. The result is that you will go from experiencing chaos and frustration to making energetic and measurable daily progress on your most important goals. And along the way, you will learn the secrets to doing the following:

- Easily align your life with your dreams.

- See measurable progress toward your goals.

- Develop keystone habits that support positive change in all areas of your life.

- Experience the peace that comes with clarity.

I created the Sacred Six to provide a simple yet comprehensive system for achieving your goals and recovering your dreams. In the chapters to come I take you step-by-step from defining your dreams to creating a plan for realizing them to putting your plan into action so you can move steadily toward your life's mission every day.

THE TIME IS RIGHT

I remember when personal computing was just starting to take off. Computers were supposed to help us work less and have more time for leisure activities. I don't know about you, but my life doesn't seem any less burdened than it was back then. In fact, it seems to be getting busier every day. I find more and more tasks and responsibilities trying to take my time and steal my attention. It is harder and harder to focus on what is important.

It is time to *truly* slow down and find the right path to achieving what matters most to us. Once I gained clarity on the direction I needed to head in, my life became infinitely more enjoyable. It brought me what I know to be true success: a sense of unwavering daily peace and joy. The Sacred Six is designed to do the same for you.

If you have picked up this book, it is probably because you are tired of not living the life you want to live or you have lost the spark of the dreams you once had. Maybe you have become a wandering nomad in an ever-expanding desert of self-help ideas, with half-read books and half-finished audio courses acquiring dust on the shelves and action plans abandoned in the middle. I've been there, too, but the Sacred Six can help you end your wandering and focus on what's important to you right now.

WHO AM I?

Good question. Let's get on a first-name basis right away. I'm JB, life archeologist and modern-day Indiana Jones, without the whip or the hat. You may know me better as the MorningCoach. I've hosted a top-20 podcast on iTunes since 1997, helping transform the lives of thousands of people in more than 100 countries with my daily 15-minute program at MorningCoach.com. I have followed the traditional education route, earning a bachelor's, an M.B.A., and a Ph.D., but truth be told, it was my street education—from black eyes to near bankruptcy—that taught me the hardest lessons and led to the biggest discoveries. Through all the failure, through all the loss, I've found a time-tested program for reaching your dreams.

LET'S GET STARTED!

The key principles of the Sacred Six process are *clarity*, *focus*, *consistency*, and *prioritization*. Part I of the book gives you the crucial foundational content. The first five chapters set out the steps for clarifying your mission, values, and goals and ensuring that they are fully aligned. Then in Part II, I guide you through creating your own Sacred Six action plan and implementing it on a daily basis. Throughout the journey, I share stories of how I transformed my life using the same tools I am offering you.

Please don't be overwhelmed by the Sacred Six process. It's comprehensive but also dynamic and flexible. It will change as your life changes, and it is easily adaptable to your needs. Just take it step-by-step, and you will gain the clarity, focus, and wind to push the sail of your life in the direction of your dreams. *My* dream is to be your guide through this process.

Now it's time for you to dive in and start working on your Sacred Six so you can move steadily toward manifesting *your* dreams!

PART

I

THE
FOUNDATION

CHAPTER

1

CHANGING DIRECTION

It is a day just like any other day. There I am, sitting in my mechanical chair, in front of my old steel desk, which somehow made it through the economic collapse of the 1970s. The office is freezing cold as always, and the smell of stale doughnuts permeates the air. I have long since given up looking out my one tiny window and instead stare blankly at the gray wall in front of me.

I have to get out of here. How did I end up here in the first place?

I had so many dreams growing up. I felt a strong inner calling that said I could do almost anything I wanted to do. It was an energy, something alive inside me. I was always joyful, always looking for ways to bring that happiness to others.

My father and mother divorced when I was very young. Honestly, I don't even remember them being married. My mother worked hard to raise me, and eventually she met a wonderful man who became my stepfather.

My father was more of a rebel. He tried many entre-preneurial businesses and always had a few bucks in his pocket. Whenever I saw him, he gave me a $20 bill, and I would head off to the toy store. My mother and step-father, on the other hand, were true blue-collar workers. My mother worked in an aviation engine plant for years, putting in her time on the factory floor. My stepfather worked his way up from delivery driver to management. He was a great man, but he had a military background, which made him strict about everything. One of the les-sons he taught me was that everything has a place, and I should always put everything back where it belongs. In my creative world, however, I never put anything back. Given how rigid he was, the two of us never saw eye to eye. None-theless, I learned some much-needed discipline from him.

Running interference between my parents taught me sales skills that served me well later in life. I was always working my father, mother, and stepfather for money, car keys, and curfews. I closed some of my best deals before I turned 18.

Unfortunately, my sales skills did not help much when it came to school. I found school boring. With all the energy I had, I could never sit still. I did well when I managed to pay attention, but that was rare. At every parent-teacher conference my teachers praised my posi-tive attitude but shook their heads at my lack of focus and attention.

Finally, I escaped high school and went to college. Like many college students, I had no real direction. I was primarily learning what a party was and where to find the next one. I wasn't into course work or classrooms and only managed to squeak through after attending three different colleges. I eventually graduated from Ball State University in Muncie, Indiana, with a general studies degree. I honestly think they gave it to me just to get me out of there.

Tired of cold Indiana winters, I decided to take my buddy—a rescued German shepherd mix named Kaos—to Tucson, Arizona. I loaded all my worldly possessions, which consisted of 62 CDs (half with broken cases) and some clothes, into my old Ford Ranger pickup truck and hit the road. To this day I have no idea why I chose Tucson. I guess I heard, "Go West, young man" and took it seriously.

It was during the Tucson years that I became a self-help junkie. I had discovered Zig Ziglar's book *See You at the Top* in my teens, but that was about all I knew of the self-help world. Now I was finding a treasure of amazing wisdom. I knew I could get out of being broke, and I knew I could be somebody. I just didn't know *how*. The self-help authors all seemed to know the way, so I devoured every book I could. I read Tony Robbins, Napoleon Hill, and Wayne Dyer, to name just a few, and I started to believe I could live my dreams. (Back then my dreams involved fast cars, beaches, women, and partying.) I kept hearing the same things over and over from these masters: Set goals, work at them, keep the right attitude, and you will win. I listened.

I took a job in Tucson selling health club memberships at a local gym. It wasn't what I wanted to be doing, but it paid the bills for Kaos and me, and let me put my sales skills to work while I set about taking action toward my goals. I tried everything from inventing new products to joining multilevel marketing companies like the People Network (TPN), the Longevity Network, 2Xtreme Performance International, and VIVA America Marketing, trying to find riches and success. I thought education was the key, so I enrolled in the M.B.A. program at the University of Phoenix. (This was before it became an online university, and my classes were held on the Tucson campus.) I loved the program, as we met only once a week for four hours. My energy and focus issues were solved. I rocked my course work for two years, never receiving less than a B.

I knew in my heart that one day my dreams would come true, but I was still employed at the health club and struggling financially. Around that time I saw an ad in the paper for a sales position at a helicopter engine repair company. I couldn't contain myself. How glamorous and cool would that be, selling helicopter engine repairs! I applied, and lo and behold I got the job. With that, I entered the corporate world, making $25,000 a year.

Let me tell you, I thought I was living the high life. I signed on for a new apartment for Kaos and me, and a new car payment, and I bragged to everyone I met that I was rich. As the weeks went by, I started to realize that I wasn't rich at all. I had just been so poor before that I thought $25,000 was a lot of money.

I decided Tucson was too low-key for my energy level. I wanted music, passion, and beautiful women. So I told my employer I was moving to South Florida. The good news is that I was doing so well that he gave me a raise to $45,000 a year and said I could work from home. *Now,* I thought, *I really am rich.* That idea lasted until I realized that the cost of living in Miami was double what it had been in Tucson. The same pattern emerged: I would earn more money, thinking I had finally made it, only to realize my expenses were higher. Just like the proverbial hamster on a wheel, I was spinning around and around and getting nowhere. I had to find something that would bring me peace of mind, not to mention money. I tried inventing more products, joining more multilevel marketing companies—*anything* to make money. Nothing worked.

Finally I found another job. This one paid a whopping *$60,000 a year.* This time I *had* to be rich, right? Well, yes, life was better, but still I was not achieving my dreams. I was hardly living a life of freedom, spending my days on the beach sipping a drink out of a coconut shell with a little umbrella stuck in it. Though I continued my trek through the self-help and personal development literature, I couldn't figure out what I was doing wrong.

Meanwhile, the years went by. I got another job, and then another. I was starting to become well known in the aviation industry, and I actually achieved the magic six-figure number: $100,000 a year. I thought I *truly* had made it at that point, but once again emptiness consumed me. What was I missing?

One idea kept beckoning to me. *Write a self-help book that will change lives, just like the books you've been reading have changed yours.*

I wanted to write, and I knew I was supposed to believe in myself. Somehow I just *didn't.* It seemed impossible for me to write a book. But the dream called to me every night as I went off to bed.

I looked at my mentors—Tony Robbins, Zig Ziglar, and Les Brown—and figured that if I wanted to live the life I dreamed about, I would have to become a best-selling author and motivational speaker just like them. So I attended a Florida Speakers Association meeting and felt right at home. I had always been a good speaker. In my college classes, when we were divided into groups, I was always chosen to do the presentations.

After the Speakers Association meeting, I told my roommate how excited I was about following my dream and becoming a best-selling author and motivational speaker. All he said was, "Who would listen to you? And why give up your career on some wasted dream?" Harsh words, but I had to agree. Who *would* listen to me? I stuck with the aviation career that delivered a steady paycheck.

Right around that time I received a call from a recruiter who said he had the perfect job for me. It was right in Miami, at Aero Hardware, a $60-million company that distributed hydraulic components. I interviewed and got the job. I was to start in sales and then in a few months become director of the $12-million aviation division. Yet again I thought, *I'm rich!* I had a company car, was able to buy a nice home, and soon thereafter met an amazing woman who miraculously agreed to marry me. I was in heaven. Wasn't I?

The corporate dream I had been chasing for 15 years became the corporate nightmare. Where did it go? What had gone wrong? This nasty pattern—making more money and then acquiring more expenses; feeling amazing at the start and then realizing I was stuck once again—just kept repeating itself.

Around my 35th birthday I had a long-awaited epiphany. I was working my way through *A Course in Miracles*, when I came to Lesson 130, which emphasizes how critical it is to know your values, because they determine how you perceive life. While I had certainly heard that concept before, for some reason the message got through just then. For the first time in my life, I asked myself what was actually important to me. Was it the cars, the house, the career? No! My first value, I realized, was *freedom*. Freedom meant having the time and the money to chuck out the alarm clock and answer to myself instead of to a boss. I saw myself in a little garret writing all day and then going to the beach to relax under a coconut tree.

So freedom was my top value, yet there I was locked in a prison of an office every day. Did I really have to ask why I was miserable? My goals had been all wrong because they had nothing to do with my values. My life was totally out of alignment with what I really cared about and wanted.

I was going to work Monday through Friday. And then Friday night I would stop on the way home and pick up a 12-pack of beer and a bottle of booze and spend the weekend drinking. I would simply disappear from what most people viewed as an ideal life. I hated that job and, at that point, my life as a whole.

Something had to give, and it did.

I was sitting at my ancient desk, staring at the gray wall and pondering the fact that there was no alignment in my life, when the moment of truth arrived. I looked out my office door to see my boss, the CEO, walking straight toward me. Next to him was the human resources director, and they didn't look as though they were on a pleasure trip. The HR director was carrying more paperwork than was involved in the Watergate scandal. She deposited the paperwork on my desk and closed the door.

My boss spoke first.

"I've been looking at the travel documents, and I notice that you haven't been traveling very much," he said. I knew the company wanted me to travel to see clients and bring in new business, but I had no interest anymore.

"I've been focused on keeping everything rolling here," I said.

My boss grunted. "I don't care how things are going here. What I care about is that things are done the way that I want them done, exactly as I say."

The HR director chimed in. "We also have reports that you're telling your employees to follow their dreams," she said in an accusing tone.

"Uh, yes," I stuttered. "We're only here on earth for a short time. We should *all* live our dreams, shouldn't we?"

"*Your* job is to get the maximum out of the employee group, not to talk about their *dreams*," she said.

I shook my head, feeling defeated. "What do you want me to do?" I asked.

"I want you to run the company the way I want it run," my boss said as he pushed the stack of papers my way. "If you want to keep your job, you will have to agree to the terms contained in these documents."

I took one look at the documents and . . . well, I can't repeat what I said. I was *pissed.* I told them no way was I going to sign their #$@*! paperwork. In that moment I knew: I had a manuscript to write. It was calling my name, and damn it, I was going to write it.

I resigned on the spot.

I was scared as hell. I told myself if I really believed in all the self-help wisdom I'd been reading, it was time to have some balls and go write this book. I said my good-byes and handed over the company car keys.

Then I had to call my wife to come and pick me up. I was scared to tell her what I'd done, yet I knew somewhere inside that it was right. I was going to have freedom— my number one value. I felt something immediately align within me. I was scared to death but, in the same moment, at peace.

My wife—what a beautiful spirit and amazing woman! I met her through a mutual friend on one of my weekend escapades. I didn't speak Spanish, and she didn't speak English. Communication was tough, but we were speaking the language of love. At least, I was attempting to. Pilar was an angel to me. She did not drink or self-medicate; she just climbed. Yep, she was a mountain climber and still is. (I have trouble even watching her, let alone climbing alongside her.) I pursued her for months. I needed love, and I needed sanity. Somehow I managed to get her to go on a date with me. I didn't even need to wear a fake Rolex. She got me out of the South Beach scene, and within a few short months, we got married.

When Pilar picked me up at the office the day I quit, she was supportive, as always. When we got home, I went to work. I decided it was my time and I had my calling. I was going to write my book and become a motivational speaker, as I had dreamed. I had escaped the corporate world and was now my own boss. It was going to be *easy*.

MY DREAM COMES TRUE—OR DOES IT?

The first thing I needed to do was write a book, but not just any book. It had to be life changing and motivational, just as my mentors' books are. My life had been a struggle, but I was discovering how to find peace and become more values oriented. I thought I could help people get out of neutral and find what was important to them.

Typing away at lunch breaks and after work, I had drafted a rough structure for my book. Now I just needed to write every day and finish it, then find an editor and printer. There was no way I was going the traditional publishing route. A traditional publisher would pay me royalties of around $1 for every book sold. By self-publishing, I told myself, I could make $20 a book—and I was going to sell millions of books! Just think of all that money! I was banking in my head—which is what I call it when you think you have money in the bank before it's actually there.

I took out the last of our savings to print 5,000 books at a cost of $5 apiece. I was sure we were going to make it all back right away. We would use the income from sales to print even more books and pay our bills. Feeling pumped, I signed off on the PDF file of the manuscript, giving the printer the go-ahead to print the books and ship them to me. I even paid the printer for 250 "Special Edition" copies with a numbered inlay, which meant I could charge even more for them. I spent another $1,500 on a CD printer so I could make my own audiobook, figuring I would recoup that investment in no time. Finally, with the last of my credit, I hired a group of web designers to build my original website, glossinger.com. I was ready to roll.

Dreams do *come true!* I kept reassuring myself. I was out of that dank office. I was free! All I needed was for the books to arrive, and then the money would pour in. I knew they were going to be delivered on a Thursday, so I found a health fair that very weekend where I could sell my books. A table cost only $550 for the entire weekend.

My audiobook CDs were duplicated (never mind that I had to throw half of them away because the machine kept breaking down). The launch event was planned. My suit was pressed and ready when the call finally came: My 5,000 books were on the way!

It was one of those days you never forget. My dream was coming true: the birth of a book, something I had wanted my whole life. I was finally going to show that roommate of mine someone *would* listen to me. I was going to help change the world.

That Thursday I was eagerly awaiting the book delivery when I got a phone call from the shipper.

"You have the forklift ready?" he asked.

Forklift?

"What do I need a forklift for?" I asked, trying to remain calm.

"To get these books off my truck," he said, and hung up.

Dead silence.

I looked outside. There it was, an 18-wheeler pulling up in front of my house. Neighbors started coming out to see what was going on. Were we moving? Inside that enormous truck were crates, crates, and more crates of books. My wife jumped in to help, and over the next two hours we hauled 106 boxes of books into our home. There were boxes of books in the living room, the kitchen, the garage, and even the bathroom. Boxes were *everywhere*. I was drenched with sweat, but still I wore my Eddie Murphy–size grin. Finally, I could rip open one of those boxes and put my hands on the dream maker itself—my book.

I tore into the box and pulled out the first copy. I can't describe how amazing it felt holding that book, opening its pages. All my dreams were lying in my hands. What a feeling!

And then I saw it. A grammatical error. *Well, never mind that,* I told myself. *Every book has a flaw somewhere.*

But then I saw another. And another and another. I rubbed my eyes to see if my mind was playing tricks on me. I put the book down and picked up another copy, hoping that the first one had been some sick practical joke. The next book was the same as the first. I tore open more boxes and found they were all the same. I couldn't believe it; they had printed the unedited version! I called my printer. At first he thought I was calling in exuberance. When he heard my hysterical tone, he calmly asked what was wrong. I told him the books had been misprinted. What could we do to fix it?

Silence.

"Nothing," he finally said. "You signed off on the PDF yourself."

In my haste to get the book published and become someone, I hadn't looked closely at which PDF I sent to the printer. He had warned me to have someone check it one more time, but I went against his wisdom and gave him the go-ahead.

Joy turned to sadness, light to darkness, heaven to hell. I was an emotional mess. I had a health fair to attend in two days, a bunch of error-filled books, maxed-out credit cards, and no savings to speak of. Oh, how in that moment I wanted to be back in my stale-doughnut-smelling office, knowing I had a steady paycheck on its way!

I pulled myself together the best I could and told my wife we would be okay. I decided I would just write a note to include in those first 5,000 copies, explaining why there were so many errors. I mean, it was only 5,000 copies, right? I was going to print millions of copies of the book. I could make the corrections for the next printing. Suddenly things didn't look so bad.

I made some flyers, headed to the fair that weekend, and stood in my booth like a proud papa. As people walked by we would exchange a few words, but they kept on walking. At some point I noticed my feet were really hurting. I looked at the clock and realized that ten hours had gone by. I had sold exactly five books. By the end of the weekend I hadn't even made enough to pay for the booth. The worst part was that I had to carry all those books back to the car. Talk about a walk of shame.

I don't know how I kept my spirits up, but I did. I pinned my hopes on the website. I thought that if you built a website, thousands of people would inevitably come and buy your book. When the website went live, I had a bunch of books prepackaged and ready to ship. I stared at my e-mail, waiting for the orders to start rolling in. The first ding was the best: I had an order! I was so pumped! I looked at the order, and it was from my mother. Once again, joy turned to sadness, light to darkness, heaven to hell. Two more orders came in from family members, but that was it. I sold a total of eight books in my first two weeks of business.

Dejected, I cried.

GOOOOD MORNING!

I now had freedom, what I valued most, but I was broke. I had to do something. A friend suggested I host a morning conference call on my website—a motivational talk to get people started on their day. So I launched the morning show at MorningCoach.com. Every Monday through Friday, I started my day by saying, "Gooood morning!" to my listeners. I sat in my desk chair, with my phone held up to my ear and a microphone right next to it, recording that day's episode.

My first day I had two listeners. A month later we were up to 180 listeners. Somehow, finally, something was working. After two months, we ran into our first high-quality problem: Too many people were calling in. It seems that the 15 minutes of inspirational talk were really working for people: They were finding it more uplifting than the news and were telling their friends to tune in. MorningCoach was starting to replace AM radio. People were listening to the show while they were getting dressed or driving to work. It was making their lives better by giving them a better start to the day. Moms were having their children listen as they got ready for school. One eight-year-old even imitated my intro and posted a video of himself on YouTube, saying, "Gooood morning!" It got 11,000 views in the first few days. My enthusiasm and the positive content seemed to be resonating with listeners.

The free conference call service I was using accommodated only 200 callers, so as the audience increased, listeners were getting bounced off the call. The complaints started pouring in—in real time. I could watch the calls coming across my screen as I talked. Let me tell you, it's hard to keep your motivational energy going when you know your fans are getting progressively more upset!

My saving grace was a new thing called podcasting. Now there would be no limit to the number of people who could hear my morning talks. I continued to use the conference line, but I was also podcasting the talks on the web. Recording with a phone on one side and a microphone on the other, I looked like a low-budget jackass, but I was getting the message across. I was making people's lives better by what I said.

I figured out the recording part, but the editing was a different story. Every day, like clockwork, I would begin the call with "Gooood morning!" And every day, like clockwork, you could hear one of my listeners waking up, walking to the toilet, and downloading a stream of his own. I couldn't hear it myself, as I was focused on the call, but listening to the recording later on, it was crystal clear. I hadn't thought to *mute the listeners*. Lesson learned.

There I was, a two-finger typist who couldn't even spell the word *Internet*, but somehow I was figuring it all out as I went. Better yet, I was developing a following. I was finally focusing on what I did best and had figured out how to deliver my message to the world. (Clearly, in those early days my medium was the podcast, not the written word!) My mission was in place: to develop financial independence and help people find peace and joy, while making the world a better place to live. I had always believed that we can change the world, one person at a time. I just needed efficient systems to make my business work.

My approach was not without critics. One reviewer wrote, "This joker thinks he can change the world one person at a time in 15 minutes a day." I'm sure glad I didn't listen to that guy.

THE $250,000 IDEA

At night I was still reading a ton of self-help books and listening to self-help audios to gather information for my shows. I found *Wisdom of the Ages* by Wayne Dyer especially inspiring. It has the same premise as my show: daily wisdom to change people's lives.

But the biggest motivator came the night I found an old tape set in a box in my closet. It was called *Lead the Field* by Earl Nightingale, a radio personality and motivational speaker. Recorded around 1960, it was one of the first personal development tape sets ever produced.

I went out to the garage and dug through the boxes to find my old Sony Walkman cassette player. Back inside, I lay down on the sofa, popped the cassette into the Walkman, and heard Earl Nightingale's deep, endearing radio voice coming back at me. He was so easy to listen to!

I had most likely listened to that same tape 20 years earlier, but I didn't remember it. I was just on the verge of being lulled into a nap when Earl started telling a story that made me sit up and take notice. It was a story that would change my life; it became the foundation for the Sacred Six.

The story was about a meeting between the steel baron Charles Schwab and Ivy Lee, a PR consultant. Lee was offering tips on how to manage the business better, when Schwab stopped him.

"What's needed is not more knowing, but a lot more doing," Schwab said. "We know what we should be doing. If you can show us a better way to get it done, I will listen to you and pay you anything within reason that you ask."

Lee told Schwab, "I will give you something in twenty minutes that will increase your efficiency by at least fifty percent." He then took a blank sheet of paper and asked Schwab to write down the six most important things he had to do the next day. Schwab did as instructed; it took him three or four minutes.

"Now," Lee said, "number the items in order of importance." Once again, Schwab did as he was told, which took another three or four minutes.

After that Lee told Schwab, "Put that piece of paper in your pocket and first thing tomorrow morning, take it out and start on item number one. Don't look at the others, just number one, and stay with it until it is completed. Then take item number two and work it the same way, and then item three and so on until you have to quit for the day. Don't worry if you only finish one or two items: The others can wait. If you can't finish them all by this method, you could not have finished them by any other method. Without some system you would probably take ten times as long to finish them, and you might not do the items in order of importance.

"Do this every working day," Lee continued. "After you have convinced yourself of the value of this system, have your men try it. Try it for however long you like, and then you can send me a check for whatever you think it is worth."

The entire conversation took around 30 minutes. The story has it that Schwab later sent Lee a check for $25,000 (around $250,000 in today's money). Along with the check was a letter saying that the idea was the most profitable lesson Schwab had ever learned. According to the story, the plan was applied over the next five years and was largely responsible for turning Schwab's little steel company into one of the largest in the world.

I leaped up from that sofa as if a bucket of ice-cold water had been dumped on me. *Wow,* I thought. *Simple but effective. Focus on one idea at a time and prioritize. I can do that.*

THE SACRED SIX PROCESS

My life started to come together after I listened to that old Earl Nightingale tape. I became more efficient through daily focus and setting priorities. That was a great start, but I had to take it a step further, because underneath my lack of focus and scattered priorities was an even bigger issue: *lack of clarity.*

When I ask myself what issue most of my clients and listeners are facing, it's just that: lack of clarity. So many of us lack a clear purpose. We live in an age of distraction. Every day we're bombarded with e-mails, tweets, instant messages, texts, phone calls, and whatever other technologies they come up with. Is it any wonder that at the end of the day we find it hard to maintain any focus at all, never mind focus on what's most important to us? We need to get our values in order, along with clear goals that are aligned with our purpose. The Sacred Six process is designed to help accomplish that. What's more, it also contains the key to making the leap from theory to practice, outlining daily actions that will keep you motivated and focused and allow you to align with divine energy. Divine energy is the power that flows through all life, connecting all. Once you are aligned with divine energy, you are in the flow of life. Ideas just come to you, along with how to act on them. Miracles occur.

The Four Ingredients

There are four main ingredients in the Sacred Six process: alignment, mission, values, and goals.

Alignment: Alignment is both the culmination of the process—a result of your mission, values, and goals working together to take you to your dreams—and the state of mind in which to begin the journey. Understanding the way alignment works is the key to the process. Alignment is what is going to keep you moving forward: It sets the direction you are going; it lays the tracks for your train. If you were to throw the wrong switch, the trains would crash. Being out of alignment is like a life full of train wrecks.

A lack of alignment is one of the major problems in the world today. Most people are distracted and living scattered, directionless lives that are not moving them closer to their dreams. If your goals are not aligned with your mission or values, they will leave you dissatisfied and unhappy, even when you achieve what you set out to do. While I was slaving away in corporate America, all I wanted was to be free. I was making a lot of money, which was one of my goals, but I had no freedom, my number one value. How was I supposed to be happy if the thing I wanted more than anything else was missing from my life?

Achieving alignment in your life is not a linear process, and it will vary for each individual. For purposes of explanation, I suggest that defining your mission is the first step. For some of you, discovering your values will precede finding your mission. That's okay. There is no right or wrong order in this process. What's essential is simply to establish your mission and values.

Mission: One of the key steps toward living the life of your dreams is to identify your mission—your purpose, or what is driving you at this moment. A mission can be as lofty and overarching as finding a cure for cancer or as intimate as communicating better with your kids. In my case, I had to start by taking a deeper look at how I was living. *What was the next experience I wanted to have? How did I want to feel?* I believed I was destined to help people; I just didn't know *how* I was going to do it. Then I felt a calling to write my first book. I thought all I had to do was write the book and get it printed, and everything else would unfold from there. Clearly that wasn't the case. Nonetheless, I remained sure I had found my mission: to help others, just as my mentors had helped me.

Many of us are waiting for the archangel Gabriel himself to come down and hand us our marching orders. Most of the time, mission is much less dramatic than that. For me, mission was more a whisper than a roar—I just knew intuitively the next right thing to do. Your mission doesn't have to be your overall life purpose—though for some people it might be. And it isn't carved in stone: Mission is fluid, changing as you and your life change. I prefer to think of mission as simply *the next experience or set of experiences you want to have in your life.*

Whatever your mission, the point is that it calls you to slow down and identify your real purpose. *What are you moving toward?* It took me a while to grasp the importance of that question. Even now, I have to check once a month and ask myself, *What am I moving toward?* The answer tells me whether or not I am still on course.

Values: Knowing your mission is only one part of the alignment equation. The other driving force is what you value. As you consider what you are moving toward, you need to ask yourself, *What are my values? What is important to me?* Values are a huge component of a good life. So why have so few of us ever analyzed ours? People spend months planning their weddings, which last for one day, yet they take no time at all to organize their *lives.* So you need to examine what's truly important to you. My own values are spirituality, family, freedom, prosperity, and peace. Yours may be very different. Keeping my values at the forefront of my mind helps me keep my life in alignment. My values help me make decisions, help me live an abundant lifestyle. Values are critical: Raising your awareness of your values keeps you moving toward the life you want.

When I am faced with a decision, the first thing I do is make sure that what I decide is aligned with my values. Because freedom is one of my top values, I have turned down a number of business opportunities that offered a lot of money but were ultimately constraining. I have also worked hard on learning to trust my intuition in decision making. Now when I have a gut sense about a decision, I run it by my values to make sure my intuitive feeling is consistent with my inner truth.

***Goals*:** The breakdown of alignment normally happens at the mission or values stage, but it is at the goals stage that you can actually start to *see* the misalignment. When I work with new clients, the first thing I ask them about are their goals, because most people have goals and can tell you what they are. Once I have their goals in hand, I ask to see their mission and values. Often I get a blank stare in return. From what I can tell, 95 percent of people have not identified their mission or values, which makes alignment impossible, since you can't align your life without knowing who you are and what you want. So, the first assignment I give clients is to identify their mission and values. That tells me who they are. Then we can compare who they are with their goals and see what changes they need to make to bring their goals into alignment with their mission and values.

In my youth, my goals had a lot to do with money and partying, which meant I was incredibly out of alignment with my mission to help people and bring positive energy into the world, and with my core value of freedom. I kept taking promotion after promotion to attain my money goal, but a more appropriate goal would have been to find work that generated revenue and also provided freedom and helped people. Thankfully, that is exactly the type of work I'm doing today.

Once you gain clarity on the four ingredients of the Sacred Six process, the next step is to put them together. For this to work, you need to build belief—belief in yourself, belief that what you want will come into your life, belief that the past does not equal the future. And then you need to move into action. You can start to manifest the life of your dreams through belief, but action is critical to fully inhabit it.

This is where the daily Sacred Six process comes into play. Around the time I listened to Earl Nightingale tell the Ivy Lee story, I had already started working with the four ingredients. After many years of fumbling in the dark, I was finally clear enough to be aligned with my mission and values. But I did not have the final piece of the puzzle. Armed with Lee's wisdom, however, I was ready to take calculated action and start moving toward my dreams. What I discovered were the steps I outline in Part II, "Into Action."

I had spent many hours in the library, researching esoteric knowledge. Then I finally found what I had been looking for all along. Every battle, every mistake, every failure in my life have led to what I have laid out in this book: a system that allows you to develop new keystone habits, feel hopeful, and find the peace that comes from clarity, while making measurable progress toward your dreams.

The Sacred Six process is simple but not easy. It is going to take you into some deep territory, as if you have opened a new tomb in a pyramid in Egypt—the pyramid of knowledge. I encourage you to relax and let the light of awareness shine into the dark realms where wonderful treasures await. Just as if you had uncovered a chamber filled with gold, you will feel wonder and peace of mind as you find alignment in your life.

So pick up your shovel, turn on your head lamp, and let's start down the pathway to recovering your dreams.

CHAPTER

2

ALIGNMENT

Finished with recording my morning podcast, I sip chamomile tea to warm my throat as I look out at the beautiful South Florida morning. Almost in a meditative state, I turn to see my wife bringing me a large manila envelope.

I still get excited when I get a package in the mail. It feels a little like Christmas, and the small child in me wants to rip open the package. Inside the envelope is a six-page letter, handwritten on parchment paper. It looks as if someone has really taken his or her time with it, so I am not going to speed-read this one. There's something very important in here; I can feel it.

"Dear JB," the letter starts, "I just wanted to tell you how thankful I am for your MorningCoach podcast. I don't think you know how much of an impact you are having on the world." I stop reading and take another sip of tea. I've received a lot of thank-you e-mails, but never a handwritten one quite like this.

As I continue reading, it sounds as though the writer has a pretty good life. She married the love of her life, and they have two beautiful children. She talks about how she built her career and how her husband has been building his. All this gives me a warm feeling, but I don't get why she sent me such a long letter.

Then I turn to page 2, and the horror begins. Like a freight train, the details come at me: the physical and verbal abuse she and her children have suffered at the hands of her husband. Her prince had become her nightmare. As I read page after page, I have to sit back to take it all in. I can feel her pain, her sorrow, her suffering. At the same time I can't help but wonder, *Why doesn't she just leave him?*

As I continue reading, however, I start to understand. She is fearful of the consequences. Where would she go? How would she live? What about the children? She is scared, beaten, frustrated, and whipped. Her soul is empty, her life devoid of dreams.

There her story breaks. "Then one day I found you," she writes. She describes how the only solace and positivity in her life was my 15-minute MorningCoach podcast. She would go into a closet and listen to it every day to find strength and hope. Then she tells of learning about the Sacred Six.

I pause after reading this. Having coached thousands of people, I am normally the optimistic one who believes anyone can change their existence and live the life they want. At this point in the letter, I can't help but think, *JB, your stuff had better work!*

The writer goes on to describe how she applied the Sacred Six to start building belief in herself and to work on her plan for escape to freedom. She tells how she took all the money she had and bought three one-way tickets from Europe, where she lived with her husband, to Los Angeles. One day she simply picked up her children and left while her husband was at work.

Her hardships didn't stop there. She was suddenly on her own with no support, no help, and no money. She endured a lot as she tried to find a job, a place to stay, and a school for her children, while dealing with her fear and feelings of isolation and loneliness. All during that time, she continued to pay to be a member of the MorningCoach.com community and download my MorningCoach podcasts four days a week. The Monday broadcast is free to all listeners, but the letter writer said that listening to the four remaining broadcasts each week was worth the investment. (In addition to the broadcasts, MorningCoach.com members have access to special courses, community forums, and other tools.) She knew in her heart, she wrote, that the Sacred Six process was going to work for her. And then she closed the letter with these paragraphs:

> I am writing this from the beach, and I just want to tell you how much I want to thank you. Yesterday I ran my first marathon, and as I finished the race both of my beautiful children were at the finish line. I felt that running this race was a lot like my life. I kept thinking about what you said: "Stick with the small steps, focus on the plan, work the plan." That is what I did, step-by-step, and there I was with my two children, celebrating one of the goals I had set for myself.
>
> As I sit here recovering on the beach, I now have a new job, a new relationship, a new life. My children have seen strength and how to overcome the darkest days. They have seen me go from cowering in a closet, beaten and scared, to being a champion. I still have

many things to do and lots to learn, but I have done it: I have become free.

It works, JB, and I thank you for the life that I now have with my beautiful children. Without you, I don't know if I would have made it. Much love.

"Wow," I cry aloud. I really don't know how to take it in. I fold up the letter and put it back in its envelope as a massive wave of peace and joy washes over me.

WHY DON'T WE DO WHAT WE LONG TO DO?

That brave woman who wrote me was able to break free from the recurring patterns that were holding her back, but how did she do it? How can we all do it in our daily lives? We may not have suffered abuse, but each of us has our own quiet challenges to overcome.

Thoreau famously said, "The mass of men lead lives of quiet desperation," and I find it hard to disagree. Most people are not happy. They don't wake up and love their lives. They are in a constant state of want.

Why? Because of the conditioned patterns we fall into in our daily lives. To understand how deeply these patterns imprint on us, imagine that you are in Colorado for a ski vacation. It's a crisp, clear December day. Picture yourself at the top of the ski slope, looking down the white-powdered mountain. You are the first skier on the slope that day, so there aren't any tracks in the snow. You grab your poles and push off. Down you go into that awesome white powder, jumping, twisting, turning as you descend. At the end of your run, you think, *That was awesome! I have to do that again!* So back up the ski lift you go.

When you return to the top of the mountain, something has happened. There are now tracks in the snow from your previous run. Still, you fly down the mountain again, following your own tracks. When you go back up the mountain a third time, you see that the tracks are now deeper. As the day goes on, the tracks deepen into ruts. You try to steer out of them, but you can't. You're stuck in the ruts.

This is what happens in life. As we continue to think in certain ways, we create ruts in our mind. We develop mental patterns that become habitual. And over time it gets harder and harder to get out of those mental ruts and change our thinking, never mind our lives. Even more insidious is that we are not the only ones creating those ruts in our minds. There are countless marketers, advertisers, colleagues, friends, and family members helping shape our thoughts so they can get us to buy their products or adopt their beliefs. This repetitive thinking can be very frustrating. Just as in the movie *Groundhog Day*, the same things keep happening to us again and again. This, my friend, is quiet desperation.

It is also one of the reasons we don't get stuff done. Once we get locked into habitual thinking, we have trouble stepping outside the box. One of my favorite TV commercials from the 1980s is for Dunkin' Donuts, with the guy who wakes up in the morning, puts on his clothes, brushes his teeth, and then walks into work saying, "It's time to make the donuts." He does the same things at the same time in the same way every morning. I have felt that way many times in my life, waking up, going through the same motions, listening to the same advice, experiencing the same conditioning day in and day out. It is a self-made prison that is difficult to escape.

So how *can* you escape the prison of your conditioning, so you can advance down the path to your dreams? It begins with a shift in perspective.

The Observer

Another trip down I-95 where the damn traffic is backed up. I'm going to be late to the office again if I don't get out of this mess. I flip on my turn signal and take the next off-ramp. It leads me into one of the worst areas in Miami, but I don't think about it because I don't want to be late. Frustrated, I take a right and head down the first street going south.

As I pull up at a red light, all I see are taillights in front of me. It looks as if I wasn't the only one with the idea of getting off the highway. I look around, trying to get my mind to settle down. Last night I read some spiritual texts about slowing the mind, so I decide to give one of the breathing exercises a shot. I know it is probably bullshit, but what else am I going to do while I'm stuck in traffic?

The idea is to focus on my breathing so I will become more present—whatever that means. In and out I breathe, trying to focus deep within my belly, as I gaze at the patchwork of gray buildings, telephone poles, wires, and bleakness all around me. In and out I breathe, waiting for Buddha himself to materialize and bring me peace. Then something weird starts to happen. No Buddha, but as I look up at the tangle of wires overhead, I see something I have never seen before: beauty in the moment. Everything slows down. Objects become clearer. The sky is a brilliant blue, and the buildings seem vibrant. The only times I've experienced anything even approaching this feeling are when I tried on a new pair of glasses and when I saw high-definition television for the first time. Everything around me is clear, bright, and vibrating with energy.

That was the day I learned the difference between the ego and the Observer. For years my life was guided by the ego. The self conditioned by culture, society, and past experience, the ego stands between my true self and the present moment. Up until that point, I had never believed in or even thought about a spiritual dimension to life. I was a man's man, a football player, and all that spiritual stuff was too New Agey for me. But there I was, in that moment, feeling immense gratitude and immense peace.

That was the beginning of understanding that truth is inside me, not outside, and in all those years when I was rushing to find gratification in the external world, I was missing what was truly most important—clarity about what was really happening in my life. I can see it all now: those years of frustration and pain, the feeling of being trapped in a self-created world, unable to slow down and get out of ego.

To this day, I think, *What a crazy place to find the truth—on some back road in Miami!* But that moment of awakening allowed me to see everything differently. It opened my mind to new possibilities, indeed to a new life. It was an unforgettable, magical moment.

After that day, I started to dive deeper into understanding who I truly am. I started to find ways to access the Observer—the true self, eternal and unchanging. I learned that accessing the Observer is essential for discovering what you really want and what you really value.

How to Connect with the Observer

There are two methods I use to get in touch with the Observer: the Mirror Ritual and Quiet the Mind.

The Mirror Ritual

Start by finding a mirror. Any kind will do, but one of those big bathroom mirrors really rocks. All you need to do is look at yourself in the mirror. Look deep into your eyes and see the being there who has never changed. It is a powerful being filled with energy, love, and ability. It is quiet, waiting to be discovered, but it is there. Regardless of how much your external appearance or circumstances change, you can look in the mirror and see your authentic self. This is the Observer.

The ego is not bad or wrong; it is just temporal. It is not going to last forever, and thus it is filled with anxiety and negativity. The Observer, however, is patient and kind. It is in no rush, unworried about its survival because it is eternal.

Understanding the distinction between the ego and the Observer is critical in helping you recognize why your life is the way it is and not the way you want it to be. If you are always living in ego as I was, then you will always be creating your reality from the ego. If, however, you can go deeper, you will manifest reality from the perspective of the Observer. That is where the power lies.

One of the secrets of life is being able to get out of your conditioned mind, your ego, long enough to discover the truth about who you really are and what you want to achieve. You don't need to summon the Observer; it is always present. You simply need to recognize it. In opening to the Sacred Six process, you are cultivating the awareness to recognize the Observer.

About now your ego is probably throwing up red flags, saying this is all a bunch of BS. That is what the ego does, especially when it feels threatened. If you are having some of those thoughts, don't worry. Let them be and keep going. The Observer isn't threatened by doubt.

Quiet the Mind

Another method for getting out of ego and into the Observer is a meditation to quiet the mind. This is a way to slow your thinking and still the mental chatter so you can connect with your deeper core. I came up with this variation on an ancient practice because people kept telling me they didn't have time to sit and meditate to find peace. Quiet the Mind takes only five minutes, but it can make all the difference in your day.

Start by finding some place comfortable to sit. Or, if you prefer, you can do this meditation standing up. I like to imagine that I'm near a cool, placid pond back home in Indiana. There's a big old oak tree there that I like to sit under to find peace. This is my private spot.

I start the mediation by going to my private spot in my mind. If you can't think of a quiet spot of your own, I'll share mine with you. (Don't worry, there's plenty of room underneath that tree.)

As you visualize your special place, make sure there is a body of water nearby. See the water as calm and placid. Now start watching your thoughts. The idea of watching thoughts may seem unusual at first, but stick with me. There is a very important purpose to this.

Think of your thoughts as pebbles. As a thought comes into your mind, picture it dropping from your mind into the calm, placid water. See the ripples radiating out from the spot where the pebble enters the water. Continue to picture pebbles—thoughts—gently dropping from your mind into the water. Don't judge the thoughts; just let them go. As the thoughts leave your mind, allow yourself to go deeper and deeper into who you truly are. Sit with the silence. In silence you can hear the voice of the Universe, or God, as you get in touch with your deeper self, the Observer.

Doing this meditation for even five minutes may be difficult at first. The more you practice, the easier it will be to connect with the Observer. What you gain is the clarity that comes from getting out of ego. And as you quiet the mind, you will be able to hear the inner voice of the Observer directing you to your next step, your next experience.

Inner Passion

My 1985 Ford Ranger pickup truck is dead. It stopped as I was going through the light. I heard a clink-clunk-clink, or was it a clunk-clink-clunk? It was something bad, and now the truck isn't working.

I am sitting on a bench, just a few yards from my stalled truck, devastated and crying. My entire net worth is sitting in the street smoking right now, and I have no idea what I am going to do.

I get up, walk over to my truck, and kick the tire, stubbing my toe in the process. Through eyes blurry with tears, I spot my journal sitting on the passenger seat. I grab it and walk back to the bench.

I have just noticed how hot it is, so now I am sweating as well as crying. I open the journal and start writing: *I am f***ed.* Nasty but true. I look around; there's nothing here but the saguaro cacti looking back at me. What a horrible situation. Maybe it's time to give up and go back home. I think about all the success books I've read and tapes I've listened to. *What bullshit,* I think. *Here I am, broke and with a truck that doesn't run, so I can't even get to work. I have tried all this personal development stuff, and nothing works. I still feel so alone.*

At that moment I start to write. As if automatically, words appear on the page: *What would a winner do?* I think, *Wow, where did that come from?* I lean back on the bench and stare into the desert, wondering what a winner would do.

Once I get past feeling sorry for myself, a positive attitude starts to emerge. Those books and tapes must have had an effect on me after all! I walk to a pay phone and call a buddy, who arranges a tow truck for me. To my amazement, this frustrating event rekindles my desire to help others just like me.

Now, 20 years later, I'm at 38,000 feet, flying home to Florida from the house in Bogotá, Colombia, we bought to be near my wife's parents. I'm writing a book and helping thousands of people all over the world with my podcast. I'm doing exactly what, as a 25-year-old kid, I imagined doing, though at the time I had no idea what a mission was.

My 25-year-old self and the woman in Los Angeles who wrote me that letter had something in common. We knew what we wanted to do, but we faced challenges going forward. We had no idea how to even start down the path toward what we wanted. We just knew where we wanted to end up.

Throughout the Sacred Six process, the Observer will be your most reliable guide, connecting you to the inner passion and energy that will move you toward your dreams. Now that you understand the importance of the

Observer, you can do what is necessary to get into that state so you can proceed with clarity to the main areas of the Sacred Six—mission, values, and goals.

CHAPTER

3

MISSION

I walk downstairs, grab my lemon water, and hit the start button on my MacBook. It fires up, programs flashing as they open, and then *POW*. I stare at all the e-mails: 101 just since last night. Time to start hitting the delete button, but as I do, one e-mail catches my eye.

Subject: Can't wait to tell you the good news.

I open it and see that it's from a MorningCoach member, Ginelle Mills. Ginelle is a stay-at-home mother with three beautiful daughters. She has always been a positive and giving member of our community.

I start to read her e-mail with excitement. Ginelle tells me about taking one of her girls to the park on a very hot day in California. When she set the child down on a swing, the baby's bare leg came into contact with a piece of metal that had been roasting in the sun. The little girl screamed in pain, and when Ginelle picked her up, she saw a small burn on the child's leg. I thought about how hot my car gets in the Fort Lauderdale sun. Poor baby!

Ginelle left the park that day saddened by the event. She blamed herself, even though she couldn't have known that would happen. As she went about mothering, one of the toughest jobs on the planet, she couldn't stop thinking about that day.

She had an idea. What if she had brought something with her to the park that would have prevented the accident? She scoured the Internet for a solution but found nothing.

"Here I am, a stay-at-home mother, with a problem I want solved," Ginelle writes. "I wanted to do something to protect other babies from this pain, so I decided to invent it. I would come up with an idea and make it work."

Ginelle goes on to tell how she did just that. She went out and bought the materials, hunted down vendors, and started to work on her mission to protect babies. Day by day she struggled to find time to raise money and build a prototype, but finally she succeeded. She had realized her mission and created the Cool Wazoo, a pad with a heat-repellant surface.

The story could end there, and I could go on to discuss the power of mission, but it gets even better. Ginelle continued to build her business. Many challenges arose with suppliers, inventory, and sales. Many times she thought about giving up. But being a tenacious person with a clear mission, she stayed with it.

And then one day, a few months later, I get a call from Luis, who handles the business side of MorningCoach. He tells me I need to turn on a TV show called *Shark Tank*. I know Luis wouldn't waste my time, so I shut down my computer and head into the living room to watch the show. *Shark Tank* is extremely popular in the United States. Contestants come before the panel of "Sharks"—well-known investors—and pitch their business ideas. If the Sharks like an idea, they ask for a piece of the business in exchange for funding. When this happens, it can be a major win for the contestants because it means national exposure, money to grow their businesses, and the help of an experienced business partner.

As I sit there watching the episode, to my surprise, I see Ginelle. She is standing in front of the Sharks, ready to tell her story and pitch the Cool Wazoo. I say a little prayer for her as she discusses her mission to help moms and babies and tells them that the Cool Wazoo is a must-have diaper-changing pad that also acts as a seat cover for a high chair, a swing seat, a car seat, and even a shopping cart.

She goes on to tell the Sharks that she is getting the Cool Wazoo made for $30 apiece and selling them for $32.50, meaning she is making only $2.50 apiece. She explains why quality is essential, but she says she can move production overseas to get the pads made for $11 each, which will help the bottom line. She also tells the Sharks she has already put $96,000 into the business. All this is news to me.

Ginelle tells the Sharks that she is looking for $65,000 in exchange for 25 percent of the business. I see the Sharks look at her as if she doesn't have a chance. One of the Sharks, Mark Cuban—the chairman of the HDTV cable network AXS and the owner of Landmark Theatres, Magnolia Pictures, and the NBA team the Dallas Mavericks—tells Ginelle that she has to put in more time and that she has a steep learning curve. I cringe because he was the one I was hoping would jump on board. All the Sharks are out.

I think Ginelle is done, that she will give up like most contestants do after they are told their ideas won't work. Instead she starts to get emotional, and I start crying, too. I see the fight in Ginelle as her authentic self emerges and she starts her presentation over, this time with more passion.

As the Sharks are again about to dismiss Ginelle, Lori Greiner, an entrepreneur known as "the Queen of QVC," says, "Hold on. I believe in you and will give you $65,000 for 25 percent of the business." Ginelle is ecstatic, and I am jumping up and down celebrating as if I just won the Super Bowl.

The power of mission is amazing. When you really know what you're going after, you get the motivation and passion to knock down walls. Ginelle was facing a wall, on national television no less, but she had her mission, and she wasn't going to take no for an answer. She is now president of the Cool Wazoo Company.

WHAT IS A MISSION?

Mission is one of the key elements of alignment. It's the big picture, the overall focus of your life at the moment, the starting point for what you want to achieve. Ginelle had a strong mission, something she believed in. She was very clear about what she wanted and was dedicated to achieving it.

But what if you don't know where you are headed? You may have a vague sense that you want your life to be meaningful, but what if you are like the younger me, and you have no clue what that would look like? If you are not clear about what you want in a big-picture sense, then dial it back and think of mission simply as the next experience you want to have, a day or a week or a month from now. How do you want to feel? Maybe you don't want to launch an Internet business, but you would like to be a better singer or painter or lover, or even just cook a meal that your six-year-old will eat. Maybe you want to pass your driver's test or get an A in your French class.

If you still draw a blank, then I suggest you jump ahead to Chapter 4 on values and dig into what really matters to you. You can then work backward and create a mission based on your values. Say your number one value is creativity, but you need an income. Your mission might be to find a job that pays a living wage yet gives you the time and flexibility to paint or go on a writers' retreat.

Connecting the Dots

Sometimes a clear sense of mission only emerges much later, and in the meantime you have to keep moving forward on intuition. Steve Jobs, co-founder of Apple, talked about trusting your gut in his now-famous commencement address at Stanford University in 2005. (Watch it on YouTube—https://www.youtube.com/watch?v=UF8uR6Z6KLc—if you get a chance, because I can't do it justice here.) One of the stories he told really stuck with me. Jobs quit Reed College after 6 months, but he stayed around for another 18 months, auditing classes that interested him. One was a calligraphy class where he learned all about typefaces and what makes great typography. The class had no practical application in his life; he just enjoyed it. Years later, when he was designing Apple computers, Jobs drew on what he had learned in that calligraphy class to, as he put it, make "the first computer with beautiful typography." He joked in his commencement speech that since Microsoft copied his ideas, the fonts on every PC in the world today can be traced back to when he sat in that calligraphy class.

At the time, Jobs had no clue what the calligraphy class would lead to. It can be difficult to connect the dots when you are in the moment, he pointed out. The pattern becomes clear only in retrospect.

Jobs went on to have a very clear mission. At one point he was fired from Apple by a CEO who had been brought in to grow the company. Later Apple was in such bad shape that they brought Jobs back. That was when he started to live out his mission. He had such a vivid picture of what he wanted to achieve that he did anything to make it happen. Borrowing a term from *Star Trek,* one of his colleagues called Jobs's uncanny ability to manipulate circumstances to his own ends his "reality distortion field." That included getting others on board to help make his vision real.

What if I were to tell you that you have the same power as Steve Jobs? You do. We *all* do, and harnessing it is all about alignment. That is why it is critical to get out of ego and into the Observer state as you formulate your mission and begin to work on it. The Observer is where your power lies. In the Observer state you can focus on what is truly important to you, on your inner passion, and draw toward you the people and resources you need to achieve your dreams.

A Dynamic Process

We are so used to the stereotypical view of mission as an all-powerful imperative, an irresistible and immutable calling handed down from on high, that we may fail to realize that mission, like the Sacred Six process itself, is dynamic. Your mission can change—and change fast.

Actor Christopher Reeve found that out the hard way. Handsome, charismatic, a Hollywood idol living his dream life as he worked at bettering his craft, Reeve *was* Superman. Then in May 1995, he mounted his horse to do something he loved: competitive show jumping. As the horse approached a jump, it suddenly stopped dead and refused to jump, sending Reeve flying over its nose. He hit the ground headfirst, losing consciousness and shattering two cervical vertebrae.

Everything changed for Reeve in that moment. Paralyzed from the neck down, he needed 24-hour care. His mission, his goals, everything about his life changed in an instant. His focus suddenly narrowed to survival. In time, however, his life changed again, and he released word to the media that he had a new mission: He would be a voice for people with spinal cord injuries. He traveled the world raising awareness and money for research, and he inspired millions. If you had told a young Christopher Reeve that his greatest impact would come not from his work as an actor but after a tragic accident, he probably would not have believed you.

Life is like that: It is not static—it is dynamic. And your life mission, like Reeve's, is likely to change. Events happen and realizations arise that redirect your focus.

I thought I knew what my mission was, and I will never forget the day it changed. I was at the National Speakers Association in New York City, and I sat in awe as speaker after speaker walked across the stage. My dream at that point was to be a speaker and author, helping lots of people as my mentors had helped me. But as I was listening to those successful speakers, I started to do the math in my head: 250 or 300 speeches a year. There are only 365 days in the year. *Were they ever home?* I wondered.

Suddenly it hit me. I didn't want to be a speaker. I wanted to speak when I wanted to speak and the rest of the time be at home with my family. That meant that the people I thought I wanted to be like really weren't who I wanted to be. I needed to shift my mission.

As you continue through the Sacred Six process, it is essential to be flexible, to maintain your ability to change—and change quickly—if required.

Why? is one of the most important questions you can ask yourself. When you discover your whys in life, you uncover your mission, your true motivation.

Your *Why*

For most people, not knowing their mission is the biggest source of misalignment in their lives, and it causes a lot of discomfort. There's one word that can help you with this struggle: *why*. To leave the ego and go deeper to find the source of your passion, the question to ask yourself is: *Why do I want to do what I tell myself I want to do?* I consider it the defining question of the Sacred Six process.

I am not sure what Steve Jobs's *why* was, but I can tell you that mine was to help change the world. And I imagine the *why* of that young woman in the abusive relationship was to help her children be free. When you discover your *why*, it will become your true motivation. It will help you overcome obstacles and move through those times when you want to quit. It is the power in your life. Most people never take a moment to evaluate why they are doing what they're doing. So if you really think about it, it makes sense that they would be frustrated.

For 20 years I pursued what I thought would bring me success and the life I wanted. It wasn't until that day when traffic made me slow down and take a detour off the highway that I stopped focusing on the minutiae my mind kept throwing at me and began to find my authentic self. Was it easy and pain-free to move in the direction of what I really wanted to do? No. The financial pain was acute. However, I would not be writing this if I had not taken the risk to change my life. Knowing that I was going in the right direction kept me on track.

That is one reason it is so important to have a mission: It can sustain you through those times when you think that nothing is working and you're ready to give up. The importance of a mission isn't just to keep you moving. It also reminds you of what you're moving toward.

This is where confusion lies for most people. Time after time I see them starting down a path only to realize that it's a dead end or doesn't lead where they want to go. For years I thought the road to happiness was paved with education. I had no idea that my education and career were taking me to a place of misery. My mission at the time was to be a successful businessman, but the more "success" I achieved on the job, the more miserable I became.

When I start coaching people and ask what they are going after, the answer I get most often is a list of material goals. So then we start breaking down each goal with that simple question: *Why?*

One of the main reasons people come to me for help is that they are not happy. They want more in their lives, but they lack energy or motivation. It's hard to have a more rewarding life if your focus is not where it needs to be. Imagine an archer drawing his bow to take a shot, only to have someone put a bag over his head. Is he likely to hit a bull's-eye?

Of course not. If you can't see your target, then how can you hit it? It's hard to find passion and energy if you don't understand your mission and *why* you want to achieve it.

We are here on earth to experience life. Every year, every day, every hour, is another experience. So when you look at your mission, ask yourself if it is more about experiences or things. If you have been focused on material goods—the perfect house, the perfect body, more money—or even on the perfect relationship or the perfect job, you may be missing out on what life is *really* about. I'm not saying that it's wrong to have material goals. Even the loftiest ambition will most likely require material goals to achieve it. What I'm suggesting is that you will probably find life more rewarding if you approach it from the perspective of the Observer. Enduring satisfaction comes from experiences, not from the things you own.

The Jaguar

There it is—black, sleek, sexy. The Jaguar has to be the coolest car I have ever seen. I walk into the showroom, and for the first time in my life I am not there just to ask for a brochure. I am actually shopping. All my life I have wanted a black Jag, and I am about to experience hitting another goal. A distinguished-looking salesman walks up to my wife and me, throws us a set of keys, and tells us to take it out for a spin.

I am shocked. I have never had someone just offer me the keys. Heck, most of the time dealers want me to leave, because it's clear I am just looking and not going to buy.

Maybe this guy can tell how much I want this car. I take the keys and get behind the wheel, and my wife slides into the passenger seat. I start the ignition and hear the car purr just like the namesake animal. I put the gear shift in Drive, step on the accelerator, and pull out of the car lot. What a rush! I know right then that this is going to be my car, my Jaguar.

We drive around for about ten minutes. It feels as though my chest is sticking out so far it should be touching the front window. *Proud* is the only word that describes the feeling. I don't think a Jaguar ever even passed through my childhood town of La Porte, Indiana, while I was growing up. What a moment this is. My wife and I return to the dealership, fill out the paperwork, and take the keys for real.

When we get the car home, it sits in the garage—majestic, beautiful, and mine. My wife heads into the house, and I spend a moment alone with the car. I look at the Jag and weep. The dream is coming true. I am living the life I always wanted.

Every day that follows, I get in the car and drive to work. I am so proud of it. I love my Jag. But day after day, month after month, that feeling of exhilaration lessens bit by bit. It is sad, really. I lose the joy, the love. It is not long before owning my Jag becomes just another payment, another burden. What happened? Why don't I have the same feeling? Where did it go?

The initial experience of buying that car was amazing, but was it the car I really wanted or the feeling that owning it gave me? That is the question I asked myself as every month I sat at my desk looking at the bills for the car payment, the gas credit card, and the insurance. Did I really need this car to experience that feeling? Sure, it was great to have the car. It was a lot of fun, and I loved it for a while, but why had I wanted it so badly in the first place? Why was owning a black Jaguar part of my life mission? What was so important about that?

Often we strive for things without recognizing why we want them, which is how we end up sending mixed signals to the Universe (God). We want something like a car; then we get it, but it doesn't keep giving us what we thought we wanted. The old adage "Be careful what you wish for" rings true, and we start to question ourselves. Do I really know what I want? Where is happiness? What is life all about?

Again, it is all about experiencing. That is the key. My Jaguar experience was amazing. But is it something that I *needed* to do in my life? I would say no. I could have had those same feelings, that same excitement, without owning the car. I don't need to buy something to feel something. Those emotions are mine. They come from me, not from things.

This is why it is critical to know how to live in the Observer, to be able to step back from ego and look deeply at life and experience it now. Don't let a material mission stop you from experiencing true success—peace, joy, and happiness. There is an old saying: "If you chase two rabbits, you will catch none." Mission is much deeper than cars, houses, boats, or relationships.

What do you want to experience? It's time to find out.

FINDING YOUR MISSION

The exercises that follow are to help you find your mission—your life purpose or just the next experience you want to go after. This will be the mission you focus on in the Sacred Six process. You don't have to do all the exercises. Perhaps only one or two will speak to you at this time. Try each one, and if you feel resistance, move on to the next. Most likely at least one of the exercises will feel right for you.

Start by taking a few minutes to quiet your mind. A great way to do this is doing the Quiet the Mind exercise from Chapter 2 (page 31). Slow your thoughts and just be. Let go and be open to receiving.

Who Do I Want to Live Like?

This first exercise is to make a list of people whose lives you admire—people who live the way you would like to live. One warning: Make sure you *really* know what it's like to be those people. Don't make my mistake and list people you *think* are living the life you want. I had never thought about being on the road as much as those motivational speakers are. That flew right in the face of my number one value: freedom.

Once you have your list of people, write down *why* you want to be like each one. What do they do? Why do you want to do what they do? What did they do to get there? The answers to these questions will help you find your mission and give you ideas about how to pursue it, such as following a trail that someone else has blazed. There is nothing wrong with that. In fact, it is wise. As I see it, the difference between wisdom and experience is that experience means making the same mistakes others have made, while wisdom means learning from their mistakes and not repeating them.

Envision Your Funeral

I am known as a positive guy, so what's this exercise doing here? But as Steve Jobs said, "Remembering that I will be dead soon is the most important tool I have ever encountered to help me make the big choices in life." It is one of the central truths of life, and it can motivate us to respect every moment we are alive. One of the things I point out to coaching clients is that thousands of people went to bed last night and didn't wake up, but you did. That says it all.

So this exercise is about coming face-to-face with your mortality. You are going to envision your funeral and then write a eulogy. I know this may not be something you want to face, but it is a great way to find out what areas of your life you need to be working on.

See yourself lying in your coffin, your body cold, your spirit gone. Really feel what that's like. See your family and other loved ones gathered around you. Who is there? What are they saying? Then pull back from the scene and focus on what you did and didn't do in your life. What was your life like? What were your happiest or proudest moments? What are your regrets?

This is an exercise you have to really dig down and get into. The more you can feel and visualize the experience, the more impact it is going to have on you. Think about what it means to be dead. There is no return, no chance to come back and try again. Your life is over. What would you have done differently?

Once you can really feel all this, write your eulogy. What were you known for? Whose lives did you touch? Be sure to include in your eulogy the following:

- A brief life history
- Important events and achievements in your life
- Something about your work, friends, family, pets, hobbies
- Your favorite memories

Focus on these four areas and don't worry if you get emotional. That is normal. Once you have finished writing, read your eulogy out loud to yourself. Let it sink in. Really feel your life.

Now comes the blessing: You are alive and have an opportunity to paint a different picture. What did you see was missing from your life? What do you want to add to it now?

The most important part of this exercise is deciding what mission you need to take on to add to your story. Remember, life is about experiences, and you are writing your own story. You have written a few chapters already, but it's time to add some new ones. Start by envisioning the end and then work backward.

As dark as this exercise may seem at first, as you delve into it, you will find it really profound. It will help you recognize that there is no better time than now to be alive.

In the Zone

There are times when I'm writing and the words seem to flow automatically, without any conscious action on my part. Do you ever feel as though things just work—that you don't have to try too hard to make something happen? Athletes call this being *in the zone*. The basketball seems to drop in the net on every shot; the golf ball flies straight to the cup. The zone is a great place to be, and we all have been there.

In this exercise, think about times you were in the zone, when whatever you were doing just flowed. A lot of times in life we fight so hard, only to realize we have been headed in the wrong direction. Look back and find those times when you didn't have to struggle. Write down what comes easily for you, and what you were doing when you were last in the zone. This will help you recognize what you can do effortlessly.

This exercise can also be a great way to help define your mission. If you are good at something and it comes easily to you, perhaps it should be part of your mission.

Revisiting Childhood

There is magic in going back and looking at the things you loved to do as a child. If you were to peek into my office, you would see a few toys from my youth, like a 2-XL robot, which is actually a glorified eight-track tape player. When I was eight years old it was my personal robot. I used to play with it all day. A few years ago I went on eBay and bought a fully functioning one.

Yes, it is cool to have my childhood buddy in my life again, but the truth is he has a deeper purpose. This toy takes me back to a time when I could touch innocence, when I had not been conditioned to think and act in certain ways and my life was not filled with minutiae. When I look at the robot, I am able to mentally return to that time and focus on what truly brought me pleasure and peace. One of the key points I have made about the Observer is that it is the part of us that is timeless, that never really changes. The ego may assert more and more control, but our core stays the same. This exercise helps you get in touch with that authentic core.

I have various other items around my office that also help take me back to childhood. You can do the same. Think about the toys you played with and the music you listened to when you were young, and bring some of those into your life now. The idea is to foster a connection with your past, with that time of innocence. Go back and really *feel* what you wanted to be when you grew up. What brought you pleasure and peace as a child? There may have been some rough times in your childhood, but I don't want you to go there. This exercise is about your dreams, about those times you sat up late at night, imagining how your life would be when you grew up.

It is time to bring some of that childhood enthusiasm and passion back into your life. What did you love to do more than anything as a child? What did your mother or father have to yell at you to *stop* doing? What could you spend hours on and hardly even notice the time passing? The answers could be a key to your mission.

Your Mission Statement

Now that you have worked through a few exercises, the next step is to put your mission down on paper. Reflecting on the exercises you have just done, think about what you want to go after. Look at your childhood and the things you wanted to do then. Think about the times when you have been in the zone. Review your eulogy: What else do you want to do before you die? Focus on the depth of your desire. Think about the people you admire. What do their stories tell you about how you want your life to be? All of these exercises will give you great material to work with. Write everything down; then reread what you've written. What emerges as the next thing you want to do in your life? That's your mission.

The beautiful thing about your mission is that it doesn't have to be the entire book of your life, simply the next chapter. So don't be overwhelmed by the process of identifying it and writing it down. Your mission just needs to point to your next experience. What will that be?

What is key is to keep your mission simple and understandable—a few sentences that will support your next experience. Don't just dash them off; give some thought to what you write. This is all important to you. It is the mission you are going to hold on to as you work through the rest of the Sacred Six process and create alignment in your life.

Missions to Inspire You

As you are writing out your own mission, other people's missions may inspire you. Here is the mission of a stay-at-home mother looking to move forward in her career. It is short and to the point, but you can see how it guides her in the direction she wants to go:

> *I am an amazing mother, focusing on growing and becoming the best that I can be. Every day I am moving toward my dreams with gratitude, happiness, and peace. I am financially free.*

And here is the mission of a young college student working on his computer science degree:

I am focused on gaining knowledge to make me a better programmer and also to build a dream company that will change the life of its users.

Then there is the mission of a customer service agent who has dreams of running her division and also becoming more spiritual:

I am connected to my spiritual source daily, and I am growing my skills and ideas to be able to run my division of ABC Customer Service Corp.

And here is *my* current mission:

I am changing the world one person at a time, putting positive energy into the world, building residual businesses, and creating financial freedom for my family and team. I am at peace, because I choose it.

This works well with my activities at present. It gives me the motivation to do what I need to do to move forward. When I am feeling down, I look at my mission. I think about changing the world one person at a time. When I don't want to do the day's work, my mission motivates me. I know there are people who need my help.

Your homework is to build your mission. Keep it short, to the point, and filled with energy. Make it current: Write in the present tense and the active voice. See yourself achieving your mission now.

Your mission doesn't have to be perfect. Remember, it may change, in some cases daily. The key is to focus on what drives you. Think of it as your assignment in life. Your mission will give you energy, even on down days. By taking the time to define your mission you are already ahead of millions of people who haven't even given it a thought.

Once you have your mission in place, the next step is to make sure your values are aligned with it. We turn to that subject next.

CHAPTER

4

VALUES

"Freedom!" Mel Gibson yells as he is about to be tortured in the movie *Braveheart.* I sit staring at my flat-screen, emotionally moved by this moment. I can't help but relate it to my current situation. I have my M.B.A. and the career I thought I always wanted, but here I am, miserable.

Freedom, I think. *Wouldn't that be great?* I feel anything but free. In fact, I feel more as if I'm living in my own personal hell. When I accepted my current job, I decided I should buy a house near the office. Now I am in so much debt I can't possibly leave my job. And then there's the medical insurance. If I quit, my family won't be covered anymore. Still, I keep hearing that word—*freedom*—ringing in my mind.

The next day, I wake up, slug down a cup of coffee, jump in my gray Ford Taurus (the typical company car), and head to work. It isn't that my job sucks. I am the director of a small aerospace company and sit on the company's board. I have a great salary and a decent boss. The commute is pretty shitty: Even though I live only ten miles away, with the traffic it can take as much as an hour. But it's not *that* bad. Many people dream of having a job like mine. At least that is what I keep telling myself. However, in the back of my mind: *freedom.*

Sitting at my desk, I stare at my computer and wonder how this became my life. Why do I feel this way? I feel as if everything around me is broken—broken promises to myself, broken heart, broken life. I sit back, look at the gray walls, and think there has to be a better way. *Freedom.*

Suddenly, I decide to write a list of what is important to me. I want to forget about my job, my education, the pressures of society, even my family for a moment, and just focus on *me*, not anyone else. What is important to *my* life? What is special to *me*? I start to write down a few words: security, travel, excitement, entrepreneurship, author, Internet, spirituality, faith, positive energy.

I keep writing. What else is important to me? Heat, beach, relationship, my dogs, dreams, being childlike, no rules, breaking free, having fun, focus, improvement, motivation . . . The words are flowing out of me. What a liberating feeling! *Freedom!* I write just before I put the pen down. A great surge of energy courses through my body. I feel enormous warmth in my heart, and that warmth is radiating throughout the rest of me. I am on the verge of discovery. This is one of the most important moments of my life.

As I reread the page I have just written, I have the urge to narrow the list to the six most important words. On another page I write:

1. Spirituality
2. Faith
3. Beach
4. Relationships
5. Entrepreneurship
6. Freedom

I stare at the words and then feel an urge to prioritize them. I rewrite the list:

1. Freedom
2. Spirituality
3. Relationships
4. Faith
5. Beach
6. Entrepreneurship

As I sit there looking at my list, I don't fully realize the significance of what I've just done, but I feel a kind of mental freedom.

I think about my life. I'm working 60 hours a week—on a good week—and I'm home for only about 30 waking hours. A typical week for me looks like this: Monday morning, get up at 6:00 A.M., shower, gulp down some coffee, kiss my wife, and try to beat the traffic. Get to the office between 6:45 and 7:00 A.M. and survive until 5:00 P.M., then fight the traffic home, arriving between 6:00 and 7:00 P.M. Eat a quick dinner, watch a little TV, brush my teeth, and go to bed. Repeat Tuesday through Friday. Then Friday night, go out after work and drink until life is fun again. Sleep in on Saturday, work out a bit, then get ready to go out again

Saturday night, dragging my wife with me. Drink until life is fun again—again.

On Sundays I sleep in, and if it's football season, I watch games all day and eat pizza. If it's not, then I watch movies all day. Either way, I go to bed dreading Monday. This is the pattern of my life. For obvious reasons, my marriage is breaking down. I have the dream job that has become a nightmare, and I am falling apart inside.

I stare down at my list. Nothing on it fits with my current pattern. I am a mess when it comes to alignment. I don't have a mission. In fact, I've never even thought of having one. Here I am, looking at my list of values, and they have nothing to do with how I am living my life.

That day I had an epiphany. I finally understood what was most important to me. It wasn't money or my career. It was freedom! I finally understood that this and the other values on my list were essential to my well-being. I needed to be doing something every day to align my life more closely with my values. I also realized that the decisions I had been making day in and day out were not grounded in anything I had given much thought to. I had no mission. I was not paying attention to values. I was living like a rudderless ship in the middle of the ocean, tossed in the rough seas, caught in the crosswinds.

No wonder I was miserable. At least I now understood what I cared about most. And that was the first step toward not being miserable any longer. That made me remember earlier in life working for a man who lived his values.

Living Your Values

Driving in my Ford Ranger pickup, I see the sign that reads "Desert Sports & Fitness." I am 24 years old and just out of college. I have been working as a fitness trainer for the past two months in Tucson, Arizona. I am barely surviving on what I make there and am hoping this may finally be my break. Somehow the owner of these gyms heard about me and wants to talk to me about coming to work for him.

As I walk into the gym on Pantano Street, I see rows of equipment and some stationary bikes off to my left. On one of those bikes is a large Hawaiian man with the muscles of a bodybuilder. He turns to me with this amazing smile and asks, "JB?"

"Yep, that's me," I tell him. He grabs the towel from around his neck, stops pedaling, and gets off the bike to shake my hand.

"This way!" he says, leading me to one of the offices along the perimeter of the gym. He asks me the typical interview questions, and then, to my surprise, immediately offers me a job. This is my first meeting with Frank Robles.

I start the next day. At my previous gym, I was working on straight commission, but Frank has given me my first salaried job ever. I feel as if I've made it. It won't be the last time I feel this way.

I work hard for Frank, getting to the gym early and doing my best to help him build his business. In return, I learn a lot from him. Frank takes me to have sushi for the first time and to Rocky Point, Mexico, for my first taste of the Latin lifestyle. His motto is work to live, not live to work. Frank is everything you could want in a boss.

Probably the most important thing I learn from Frank is what it means to live according to your values. I notice right away that he runs his business hard Monday through Friday morning, and then on Friday afternoon, he jumps in his truck and heads to his house in Mexico to soak up the sun and have a blast. He does this every week without fail because fun and joy are important to him. As a result, he always seems to be jovial. What an amazing lifestyle.

Years later when I looked back on my time with Frank, I wished that I had followed his lead. Instead, as I started to want more things in life, I decided to leave Frank and go back to school so I could pursue a corporate career. I will never forget the look on his face when I told him. Frank was much wiser than I ever imagined. He had probably never done a values exercise, but he knew what was important to him. He built his life, not his business. It was amazing to see the way he lived, even if I couldn't emulate it at the time.

As Steve Jobs said, you can't always see how the dots are going to connect in your life, but I can see them now in retrospect. If I had stayed with Frank, I think I would have had an amazingly free life, instead of spending 15 years in office jobs that I hated. However, if I had done that, I wouldn't be writing this book; I would probably be on the beach at Rocky Point. I may not be able to take back the 15 years that led up to my personal Mel Gibson moment when my inner self screamed, *"Freedom!"* but I can take the lessons I learned from Frank and apply them now. It's never too late. The message of Frank's life was simple: Know what is important to you, and live your life accordingly. Frank knew his values, he knew what was important, and that life lesson will stick with me forever.

Your Mental Kingdom

Stay with the job, quit the job, or take a new job? Decisions. I thought I knew what I wanted when I left Frank. After I got my M.B.A., I was offered a job selling uniforms for G&K Services. It came with a salary and insurance. Finally I was on the career path I thought I needed to be on.

The problem was I didn't know my values. I left my decisions up to my conditioning: Get the steady job with health insurance. Buy the house with the white picket fence. Wear a blue blazer and a red power tie if you are going to be someone, and don't forget the car. You have to have that luxury car, then the watch to go with the car, and then the pen to go with the watch.

I see this all the time with coaching clients—a lack of clarity about what is truly important to them. When you don't know what you value, you let others' ideas direct your life. That has to stop. It is time to control where you want to go and what you're going to do, and not let others dictate when or how you're going to do it.

I equate taking charge of your life with being the king or queen of your kingdom. If your mind is your kingdom, then you have to learn to protect it against invading forces. As the ruler, you must decide who to let in and who to keep out—which voices to listen to, which ideas to accept. It is time to start protecting your kingdom. Don't welcome intruders who are going to pull you off course.

By now you are beginning to understand the importance of getting clear on where you are headed. As a result, you may be thinking about wrong decisions you have made in the past. Maybe you left your kingdom unprotected, and you feel frustrated or confused as a result.

I've felt the same way. I made a lot of decisions based on a conditioned ego, but the good news is that the Universe (God) is always conspiring for our benefit, to get us where we need to go. I may have strayed from my path for years, but I was brought back to what I always wanted to do. If you have taken some wrong turns, think of that as part of your journey. Instead of being thrown off by it, focus on getting back on the right path.

This brings us to another key element of the Sacred Six—awareness. As you go deeper into the process, you will understand more fully how you got to where you are today. Your inability to make decisions based on your values is likely to be one of the main reasons you feel that your life isn't as you would like it to be. It's tempting to ask why the Universe (God) would allow us to veer off course. That is one of the great mysteries of life—free will. Free will gives us the opportunity to experiment, to *experience*. If you were just led down a path, how would you be able to experience life? Living means being able to learn, to create, to write your own story. Focus on that and on understanding the deeper issues that motivate you, rather than judging yourself harshly for being off track.

Wherever you are right now, you are right where you need to be. Take a moment to really feel that. What you need to do now is put your values in place so you can start making values-based decisions.

If I had known years ago what I know now, before I made the decision to leave Frank, I would have taken out the list of my top six values and reviewed them. I don't dwell on the past or judge it. We learn from our experiences, and then we leave them there and move forward. Whatever my values were back then, the two things I know for sure now are that I need to protect my kingdom and I need to make decisions based on my values.

Making decisions based on your values is about clarity, about really getting to know what is important to you as a person. If your mission is the sail that will take you to your dreams, your values are the rudder that will steer you and motivate you.

WHAT DO *YOU* VALUE MOST?

Now that you see what a key role values play in your life, it is time to start thinking about what you value most. Values aren't off-the-cuff decisions. They are revealed to you as you get to know your true self. As you do this exercise, you will need to get into an Observer mind-set to understand what is important to you.

Writing Your Values List

Think about what is important to you at this moment: a new career, perhaps, or getting your relationship back on track, or spending more time with family. Then turn to the values list in Appendix I (page 169). Go down the list and circle any words that have meaning for you. Circle as many as you want; there are no limits in this process. What's important is assembling a solid list of values that are meaningful to you.

Once you have gone through the whole list, go back and look at the words you circled. Then take the following steps:

1. Write down your top ten values. Don't worry about the order; just jot down the ten you select as the most important to you.

2. Once you have your top ten values down on paper, choose the top six.

3. Prioritize your top six values in order of most to least important.

Spend some time on this exercise and really focus. It may take some work to choose your top values, but it is critically important that you do so. Your list is going to help

---

you get clear when you are making decisions. Keep your values list with you at all times. Put it on your phone, so you can look at it whenever you want. Then if you have a tough decision to make, you can just pull out your Sacred Six list and make a choice that's consistent with your values. Once you start doing this regularly, you will live a more aligned life, with fewer bumps and a smoother ride.

Identifying your top values is critical to the alignment process. You have your mission from Chapter 3; so now take a few minutes to make sure that your mission and values support one another. If they don't, you are likely to have issues, just as I did when I was working in the aerospace industry, and my mission—to climb to the top of the corporate food chain—conflicted with my number one value, freedom. I was also out of alignment with another one of my values: maintaining my health. The constant travel for work made it hard to eat right or get enough exercise, so my body was falling apart.

The Importance of Values

What a day! I have spent it pulling weeds behind my father's tire-retreading facility. The half-hour drive home afterward is grueling in the June heat, and since this is my first summer home from college, all I want to do is party. I walk into the house, grab a Miller Lite from the fridge, and turn on the TV.

I start flipping through the channels, and every one is showing images of some guy standing in front of a huge military tank. At 20 years old, I'm not into world politics, but watching this guy as he stands on his own, blocking that tank, fascinates me. All I can think is, *What balls!*

It is June 5, 1989. The broadcaster is reporting the crackdown on protesters the day before in Tiananmen Square in Beijing. Troops had opened fire on student-led demonstrators protesting government corruption and calling for reforms. Hundreds of protesters were killed. Here on the screen, I see one man standing in front of a column of tanks, facing death. Luckily the lead tank driver stops before hitting him. The image is burning itself into my mind.

I continue to watch as the protester climbs on the tank and speaks to the commander, then climbs down and stands to the side. The tanks start up, and the guy again steps in front of the lead tank. Again, the tanks stop, and the standoff resumes. It continues until two men come and haul the protestor away.

Shocked, I turn off the TV and head to my room. Here I am, in my cozy Indiana home, getting a college education, with a tough but good summer job, while there is a guy halfway across the world risking his life. What drove him to do that? What gave him the strength and the courage? I can't even imagine the answer.

Fast-forward 25 years, and I now understand what drove him — his values. He valued freedom of expression enough to give his own life if that was necessary for the greater good of all.

To this day what happened to the protester who came to be called "Tank Man" is unknown. Some have said he was executed within the week; others have said he is still alive. The one thing I know is that I was left with deep appreciation for what he did. I will never forget the image of that unknown rebel standing in front of the tank. To have that much courage and passion is what I started striving for back then.

That was one of my first lessons in real motivation. Since then, having coached thousands of people and studied motivation for more than two decades, I understand the truth about it: I can't motivate you; only *you* can motivate yourself. Motivation arises from the internal reasons why you do things and from the values you hold. All anyone else can do is remind you of those values.

When I am speaking to an audience, my motivation is to help people uncover the values that will assist them in breaking down their inner barriers to finding motivation and taking action. Understanding your values lights the fire of internal motivation, as your authentic self comes forward. You align with your core, with the source of your strength, the authentic true self, and return to power. Breaking free of resistance releases you into a state of ease and flow. This is when motivation takes hold and you start to take action.

If motivation is external, generated by the conditioned mind, it quickly burns out. On the motivational speaking circuit, there is actually a term for this: *the suntan effect.* When you go out in the sun, you get a tan, but as soon as you spend time away from the sun, the suntan fades. This is what happens with external motivation. You go to an event, get all fired up about what you learn, but after a few days, the effect wears off. When your motivation is internal, based on alignment of your mission and values, the effect is more lasting. You have a pathway to your inner fire. Your desires are driven by a higher calling from the core of your being, not by some egoist want.

One reason many people are unhappy even when they hit their career goals is that their goals are not aligned with their internal motivations. A typical response is to blot out their unhappiness and frustration with drinking or using recreational drugs or popping Ambien to sleep. This is what being out of alignment with your values and disconnected from the Observer can do: leave you to dwell in a lower level of consciousness, the realm of competition, frustration, resentment, and hatred. At this level, you can never win; you will never be good enough by the ego's standards. It is a place of fear in which you distrust even yourself.

THE FOUR LEVELS OF CONSCIOUSNESS

As I see it, there are four levels of consciousness that we move in and out of on a daily basis. Think of them as a guide to awareness. Being aware of how you are thinking helps you move through inner obstacles and achieve clarity. Being unaware makes decision making more difficult. Familiarity with these levels of consciousness will help you understand why you are feeling a certain way and how you can move to a higher level of thinking.

The First Level of Consciousness:
Escape into Alcohol, Drugs, Movies, Books, or Sports

At the first level of consciousness, people are just looking to escape their present circumstances, so they reach for anything to help them zone out. They may drink a six-pack of beer in front of the game on TV, binge-watch movies every night, retreat into the latest thriller, or smoke a little dope—whatever will change their current state of mind. They look for freedom through escape, even though it is only a temporary fix.

A little escapism can be harmless: A good book or exciting movie can take your mind off your worries, and who doesn't love that? But when escaping is done to excess, it can become harmful, even addictive.

The Second Level of Consciousness: Daily Life, or Focus on Day-to-Day Minutiae

At this level of consciousness you are living day to day, minute to minute, sleepwalking through life. This is the level on which most people exist. Like the man in the Dunkin' Donuts commercial, they get up, go make the donuts, come home, plop in front of the talking box (television) for the evening, and then fall sleep. The next day—wash, rinse, and repeat.

Most people are imprisoned in this consciousness all their lives. It normally takes a massive wake-up call to get out of this sad state. I was at this level until I woke up that day driving to work through the backstreets of Miami. I always knew there must be something better than the way I was living, but it was not until that moment that I awakened to the possibilities in life.

The Third Level of Consciousness: Living in Psychological Time

At this level of consciousness you are stuck in the future or the past. The future is where many dreams are lost. At this level, the belief is that when the next paycheck comes, life will be great, or when you win the lotto, you will be happy. The flip side of this is dwelling in the past—living off memories of past accomplishments. Either way, people on this level are unhappy in their present circumstances and can't move forward. They are stuck in time.

The future will be here one day, but it will be on a continuum with the present. When you get past the third level of consciousness, you understand this, and you look at what you can do right now. Instead of sitting back and worrying about the future, you take action. To move through the third level of consciousness, you need to be aware of psychological time and bring yourself to the present moment.

The Fourth Level of Consciousness: The Observer

The problem with the first three levels of consciousness is that when you are in those states, it is hard to set goals or move toward a mission. You are either stuck in day-to-day minutiae or in another time, or you are trying to escape altogether. Working on goals and dreams from these states results in a lack of clarity and a lot of confusion. A much better way to pursue your goals and dreams is from the fourth level of consciousness—awareness, the awakened mind.

Awareness is the mind state of power and strength—the mind of the Observer. Living in the present moment, you can see things clearly and plan your next experience. You are able to find your path and what truly makes you happy. Aware of what is happening in your life and how you feel about it, you can focus on what is important to you. What do you want to manifest? At this level of consciousness, you are your true self. Your mission and values are fully aligned.

The Sacred Six is designed to move you into this highest level of consciousness, where *you* determine the direction of your life. This is the realm of the Observer; the ego has no voice here.

If I have an important decision to make, I don't want to be on the first level of consciousness; I want to be on the fourth. I move in and out of these levels, always striving for the fourth. I know when I am there because I feel energy and flow. I accomplish things without any drama. This is what alignment does: It ties you into this amazing flow.

It all starts with understanding your mission and values. Again, look at Steve Jobs. His father was a carpenter and believed in making everything look beautiful, even the back of a piece of furniture, which no one would see. So at a very young age, Steve learned the value of creating art in everything he did, and later his mission was aligned with his values. When he built the first Apple computers, Jobs wanted the inside to look as good as the outside, and that was a first in the tech world. Jobs actually had the technicians sign the inside of the computers they produced. This value was transferred to others and lived on at Apple even after Jobs's death. Steve Jobs's legacy and the incredible innovations of his company demonstrate the true power of values.

When you are aware of what is most important to you, and you can access the fourth level of consciousness, you can set up your mission and goals around your values. You know without question what you are moving toward is what is most important to you. As I write this chapter I am in alignment. This not only brings me freedom but also lets me help others—another important part of my mission.

Awareness of what is happening in the present moment is one of the greatest powers you can harness. You can be proactive and respond to situations, moving toward what you truly want rather than merely reacting to what life throws at you. This will serve you in many ways as you continue to recover your dreams through the Sacred Six process.

WHAT WILL YOUR LEGACY BE?

Values are what drive us forward. They help define not only who we are but also what we will leave as our legacy. Think about legacy for a moment. This is a question I often ask my new clients: *What will your legacy be?* Like the eulogy exercise in Chapter 3, this question gets you thinking more deeply about who you really are and what you really want.

There has never been a time in human history when this question has been so important. I have no idea who my great-grandparents were or what they did. I don't even know much about my grandparents and only have a few mental images of their lives. Imagine what the future will be like for our grandchildren and great-grandchildren. With the Internet and all the social media around today, even your great-great-great-grandchildren are going to know everything about you. Talk about legacy!

It is time to start thinking about what you will be remembered for. This is why the Sacred Six process is so critical. It helps connect you to your legacy, to the footprint you are going to leave. You want to leave behind what is true to who you really were.

Think about the legacy of Rosa Parks, often referred to as "the First Lady of civil rights." Put yourself in her place on December 1, 1955, in Montgomery, Alabama. Parks had worked all day as a seamstress at a local department store, and she was tired. She got on the bus and paid her fare. The first section on the bus was reserved for "whites" and the back section for "colored people," as the signs on both sections clearly indicated. Parks was sitting in the middle of the bus when James Blake, the bus driver, noticed that some white people were standing. So he moved the colored sign behind Parks's seat. That meant she would have to get up and move.

She moved one seat over to the window but did not move back behind the "colored" sign, so Blake told her, "If you don't move, I am going to have to call the police." Parks said, "You may have to do that" and refused to move. The police came and arrested her, charging her with violating segregation laws. In refusing to compromise her values— her belief in equality—Rosa Parks left an incredible legacy. She not only helped touch off desegregation efforts in the South but also demonstrated the importance of upholding your values, even in the most difficult circumstances.

That level of awareness is what the Sacred Six is all about. It can be challenging sometimes to live in the now and stand by your values, but the more you take this on day by day, the more satisfaction and peace you will experience. And you will leave an amazing legacy.

The key then is to get your values in place. It is critical that you identify your six top values and prioritize them. And I encourage you to revisit your values list every three to four months. The Sacred Six process is dynamic and flexible, and it moves with you. Your mission will change as your life changes, but values tend to be more enduring. Not that they can't or won't change, but as your ethical foundation, values tend to remain relatively constant.

Once you have your values in place, you can rely on them in all areas of your life.

Passion

I can't sleep. I'm so excited about tomorrow—like a child on the night before Christmas. I'm pumped to be alive. I grab the copy of *Don Quixote* on my nightstand and disappear into stories of my favorite gallant knight, hoping to quiet my mind. I finally drift off to sleep, only to be awakened when the alarm rings at 6:00 A.M. Rolling over, I feel an amazing sense of wonder flowing through my body. It is a new day, a new experience, a new life.

This is how I live. It is not hashing out problems that keeps me awake; it's excitement about the day to come. It may sound as if I'm on the borderline of insanity, but the truth is, anyone can live like this—and everyone should. Your days of quiet desperation are numbered once you know where you are going. Life gets really exciting.

To me, living with passion is what it's all about. I love every day, every hour, every second. If you can't get back that thrill of being alive, you are going to face challenges in bringing your life into alignment. It will be hard to find peace, and peace is critical to alignment—to connecting with your true self. This does not mean you have to run around thinking nothing but positive thoughts. It just means having some quiet gratitude for the opportunities you have been given in this lifetime.

Your story doesn't have to be as drastic as mine, but you do need to dig deep and find passion for your life and for the blessings you receive while you are here on earth.

I understand that there will be bad days. I will never forget when Kaos, my German shepherd mix, died at age

17. I did not want to get out of bed for days. Not every day will be filled with roses, puppies, and Eskimo kisses. Being present to *all* our experiences—good and bad, pleasure and pain—is the essence of being human, and there are days when we need to be totally present to sadness and darkness in order to heal.

However, even on the darkest days, you can find the flame of passion inside you and start enjoying your life. I encourage you to dream again, as you work on your values. Rekindle your passion. Don't worry about what you are going to be when you grow up. Focus on what is important to you *now* and what stirs you to action.

With the Sacred Six, you are formulating a plan to live life on your terms—to live a life based on the energy and motivation that comes from within, not on some egoist want that, once fulfilled, runs out of steam. You now have the tools to start living with true passion. Your mission is set. You know your top six values. Now your focus will shift to your goals and to bringing the experiences you want into your life. It is time to make your dreams a reality.

CHAPTER
5

GOALS

I know something is up. I am being called into the CEO's office, which is usually not a good thing. Gene Kraay—a Vietnam veteran, F-4 pilot, and soccer goalie—is no one to mess with. You know you're in trouble when he stops speaking to you; that is often the first red flag. I've been called in, and I'm pretty sure I know what he wants to talk about. So I gather up my notebook and walk down the hall to Gene's office.

I have been working at Pueblo Airmotive, my first real corporate job with benefits and a salary, for three years. I got the job after seeing an ad in the *Tucson Citizen* for a helicopter engine repair salesperson. I didn't have many sales skills, but I figured what the hell and gave it a shot. I even wrote a letter to both Gene and Dwight Cox, the vice president of the company. I didn't know it at the time, but Gene is an accomplished writer, and my writing then was horrendous. During the interview, Gene and Dwight liked my energy and laughed about my letter. They decided I was their guy even though I was 26 years old, fresh off selling health club memberships, and had no experience selling helicopter engine repairs. So I got my foot in the door and went to work.

Gene; Dwight; John, the head of sales; and I had sales meetings every Friday at which we would report on what we were working on. I had some experience setting goals but never at a corporate level. I loved watching Gene put his spreadsheets together, showing where we were going and what our goals were. He was organized and meticulous in his metrics. It was in these meetings that I started to understand the power of goals.

In the beginning, the goal set for me was to bring in one Huey Helicopter engine for repair every two months. So that was my focus: getting engine repairs into the shop. My territory was the East Coast, and one of the accounts was the NASA Kennedy Space Center—yes, *the* NASA.

One day soon after I started the job, I was sent to NASA because a spur gear—a tiny gear in the Huey engine—was vibrating and breaking, causing engine failure. At least that was what I had been told. My knowledge was very limited at that point, and I didn't really understand the details—a fact I was keenly aware of when I arrived at the meeting. Sitting at the table in front of me were about 20 NASA scientists. I swallowed long and hard and nervously sat down. The scientists immediately asked for my thoughts on the Huey engine's problem and how my company could fix it. Sweating and shaking but with all the strength I could muster, I did what I had always done: I was honest with them. I said, "I don't know."

They all looked at me as though they were wondering why I was there, until one of the engineers finally spoke up. "Well, that is refreshing," he said. "Every other person we have had in here just talked some theories and a bunch of BS. At least you're honest." I gulped and said, "Thank you." Then I told them, "I don't know, but I know someone who does. He's the first engineer on this T53 engine, and he has signed on as a consultant with our company. I can make a quick call to him now."

For the next hour, the consultant and my company's engineers spoke on the phone with NASA's scientists in technical language, most of which flew right past me. At the end of the conversation, the head engineer for NASA stood up, shook my hand, and said, "Nice job. Get me your proposal by this afternoon." I hand-delivered it later that day, and the head engineer looked it over and signed it. Repairs for four engines! I had hit my goal plus three. What an amazing feeling! I was so pumped I danced all the way back to my car.

Gene taught me about the power of goals, but by the time I'm summoned to his office, I've become bored with Tucson and have come up with some new goals of my own. I have just been on a sales trip to Miami, where I put together a proposal to work for Gene. As I approach his door I am really worried about that proposal. In my youthful arrogance, I wrote that if he wouldn't let me do it, I would go work for McDonald's. I don't know if you have ever had the feeling that you have just done something very wrong, but that is how I am feeling at this moment.

I walk into Gene's office, and there he is, hammering away at his computer. All I can see is the back of his chair. I have so much respect for Gene, and I don't want to let him down, but I need a change and have set that as my personal goal.

"Sit down," Gene tells me. I sit and wait for him to turn around. I am sure by now that this conversation will not go well, and I am prepared to end my career.

To my surprise, Gene turns around in a pretty cheerful mood.

"Miami," he says. "Great place. You're going to need more money if you want to live there, so I'm going to bump up your pay. But if you do this, don't screw me. You're going to need to make me some sales."

My jaw drops. I don't know what to say.

I knew I could make it in Miami on my own, but Gene's faith in me helped a lot in getting me where I am today. Still, I had the same problem with the new job that I had back when I worked with Frank Robles—a lack of alignment. I understood how to set and hit goals, but I didn't yet have my mission and values in place to ensure that my goals were taking me in the right direction. I hadn't put it all together yet.

Like a magic hand pushing me forward, the Universe (God) kept me going, and eventually I learned how important it is for alignment to put your mission and values in place *before* you set goals.

WHAT ARE GOALS?

We are going to delve deep into goal setting, since it is one of the fundamental areas of the Sacred Six process. The first step in setting goals is to really understand what a goal is. When most people think about goals, they think about material things like *I want a million dollars, a ten-bedroom house on the beach, and a Rolls-Royce.* Those are not goals, however; those are wishes. A wish is something that goes beyond our current state of thought or capacity. We make wishes when we have not done the internal work that achieving a goal requires. There is a place for wishes—or, more accurately, for what I call *stretch goals*—in the Sacred Six process, but the main focus is on *mission goals*—those that move you in the direction of your mission, the focus of your life at present. Depending on what you want to accomplish, a mission goal may also be a *career or business goal*—a work-related target that helps you move forward professionally—or a *personal goal* in an area like relationships, family, psychological growth, spiritual practice, or hobbies and interests. *Stretch goals* are those that move you out of your comfort zone, challenging you to aim for something that's a long shot or feels scary to pursue. Unlike a wish—magical thinking that yearns for life to be a certain way—a stretch goal is reachable if you are willing to work toward it. It stretches you past your current thinking.

The point is, you can have unlimited goals. Even if they don't fit with your current mission, you don't have to let them go. You just have to prioritize your goals, deciding which ones fit with your mission at present. In the Sacred Six process, six is the maximum number of goals we can pursue at any one time. The rest can remain on hold

Setting goals starts with revisiting your mission and figuring out what you need to do to get there. Look now at your mission statement. What are the steps required to achieve your mission? The mother whose mission is to improve her relationship with her teenage daughter might, for example, set a goal of starting a conversation with her. Another goal might be going on a vacation together. We could easily list a number of goals that would support the mother's mission of strengthening the mother–daughter bond.

Or consider the man who at the age of 33 decides to look for the love of his life. One of his goals might be to join a club focused on activities he enjoys. Another goal might be to post his bio on an online dating site. There are dozens of different goals he could set to move toward his objective of finding love.

The Power of the Pen

Goal setting is a hot topic these days, and there is a lot of information available on the subject. In my coaching and speaking practice, I often find that most people don't write down their goals. People I've worked with may have thought about goals, but thinking about them was where they stopped.

Failing to focus on your goals is like trying to thread a needle with your eyes closed. You're not going to get the results you want. If you don't focus on them and write them down, you are probably not going to reach them.

One of the tools I like to use in goal setting is a journal. Over the years, I have written my goals in a journal. I write in a very basic way, just jotting down a few words about what I want to accomplish. I'm amazed to look back and see I've achieved almost every one of those goals. And we've all heard stories of people who have a bucket list—a written list of things they want to do before they die—and have successfully ticked off most of the things on their list. When I was younger, I wrote a list of 100 things I wanted to achieve, and I have already crossed off 84.

The first thing I do when I sit down with my journal for a goal-setting session is quickly review my mission and my top six values. Then I relax my mind to get into the Observer state. I am seeking clarity, and I want to be totally present, not wallowing in the past or projecting into the future. I then start to write down my goals.

Setting Your Goals

Now it's your turn to work on your goals. Be sure to leave yourself enough time to consider deeply what you want. I suggest you use the following process:

1. Start by working backward from your mission.
Look at your mission and ask yourself what you need to do to get there. Go ahead and write down as many goals as you want. Later you will see how the Sacred Six process comes alive when you prioritize them. After you list your goals, review each one, asking yourself if it is really something you want to experience at this point in your life.

2. Write down what you want to bring into your life personally and professionally.
This may become a long list of things you want to accomplish. If you really believe in them, your belief will keep the energy flowing to make them happen.

3. Think about your stretch goals.
These are the fun ones, the blue-sky goals. You can really let your imagination go with these. They can be as impractical or improbable as you want. Just be sure to write them down. They may become Sacred Six goals someday.

As you work on your list of goals your focus will probably be on the challenging ones, but don't forget to include the fun goals. Goal setting should be an enjoyable process that flows freely, as you think about what you want to accomplish and what you will need to do to achieve it. With fun goals, you can let your imagination fly. Who knows? It may be a blue-sky goal that motivates you to keep going.

It is important to keep in mind what makes a goal good. There is an acronym that has been around for decades in the business world that can be really helpful in this regard: SMART. For a goal to be good, it should be:

- Specific
- Measurable
- Attainable
- Realistic
- Timely

Specific means you have to be as precise as possible about your goal: what it is, why you want it, and how you plan to reach it. In his book *Think and Grow Rich,* Napoleon Hill explains that you can't just say you want money; you have to say what you are going to use the money for and what you will do to bring it into your life. So be as specific as you can. If you want money, how much do you want? When do you need it? What do you plan to do with it?

You also need to make your goal *measurable.* This is one of the principles I learned from Gene Kraay: Everything, including goals, needs metrics around it, so that you can measure your progress. If your goal is to increase your income by $5,000 a month, then you can measure your progress by tracking how much more you are bringing in each week, knowing that you will need to generate, on average, an extra $1,250 a week to reach your goal. You can take this even further and break it down into how much more you will need to make each day—an extra $250. Those are your metrics.

The *A* is about making sure your goal is *attainable*. Do you believe it is possible? A goal can be challenging; in fact, it's good if it forces you to stretch a little and rise to the occasion. But it also should be doable. There's no point in pursuing an unreachable goal.

While *attainable* means you believe the goal is within your ability, *realistic* means the goal is achievable with the resources available to you at present. *Attainable* and *realistic* are similar as they both relate to belief. Is the goal you have chosen really something you can make happen? You need some stretch goals, but if you don't believe your goals are attainable and realistic, you are unlikely to achieve them. Adjust them until they become objectives you believe you can meet.

Timely means you need to determine how long it will take to achieve the goal. That means setting deadlines so you take action toward reaching your goals and they don't remain goals forever. This is an important part of most goal setting, although I have a few stretch goals that I don't have a timeline for.

Visualizing Your Goals

As you are working on your goals, one helpful—and fun—tool is a *dream board*. This is a board or poster with images representing your goals. Building a dream board is an activity I learned the skills for in kindergarten, and it still serves me well. I like to gather magazines and cut out pictures related to what I'm after. (You could also search for images online and print out pictures from there.) Then I take a piece of white poster board and some glue and go to town making a collage. It is motivating to look at your dream board every day and visualize attaining your goals.

Visualization has power. Consider how well it worked in one actor's life. One night in Hollywood, California, he was broke and feeling desperate. His dream of becoming an actor just wasn't working. He went on casting calls and interviews with directors but failed to get callbacks. Over and over, he was told no. Rejection is part of every actor's life, but he wondered if he was being myopic to stick with it. In his mind he kept repeating, *Maybe I should just give up.* Still, he continued to dream about what it would be like to be a great actor one day.

The actor had heard about the power of visualization and decided to give it a try. He wrote himself a check for $10 million, dated it Thanksgiving 1995, and in the memo line wrote, "For acting services rendered." He folded up the check, placed it in his wallet, and continued to go after his dream. Earning $10 million was a stretch goal for sure, and even his dream of being a paid actor seemed like a long shot at times. However, he had a mission. And his values and goals were in alignment.

Finally, around Thanksgiving 1995, Jim Carrey got the call for his first $10-million dollar job! You may be skeptical and chalk the amount up to coincidence, but I have seen results like this time and again. This is the power of having a solid mission and clear goals. Carrey had the fire inside to keep pursuing his dream, and despite being rejected day after day, he believed he would eventually succeed. The day he wrote himself the $10-million check he started a chain of events that led to hitting his goal.

Why and Goals

Coming up with your goals list is step one in goal setting. Making sure your goals are aligned with your mission and values, as Jim Carrey did, is step two. Goals are powerful. They are the steering wheel that guides your drive through the journey of life. As you think about your goals, keep in mind that one of the most important principles in good goal setting is understanding *why* you want to achieve that goal in the first place. Always remember to look at your goals and ask yourself, *Why do I want this?* The answer may change your whole life.

You may want something but find out you want it not for the reasons you think—like that Jaguar I was so desperate to bring into my life. If I had sat back and looked at *why* I wanted it, I might have realized that it wasn't really the Jaguar I wanted. What I wanted was approval and respect. I wanted to feel important. It really had nothing to do with the car.

Say you have been lusting after the latest designer handbag—something to make you feel cool, one of the in crowd. Do you really need a designer bag to feel that? When I work with people, I find that material goals are where a lot of breakdown occurs. I simply ask *why* they really want something and then listen to the response. More often than not, when they really examine their reasons, there goes another thing off their list! So as you are making your list of goals, be sure to include the reasons *why* you want to accomplish each one.

Many people don't know how to set goals. If they set goals at all, they often set the wrong ones—goals that are not aligned with their missions and values. This is where the Sacred Six process can help. Instead of rushing toward goals you later realize are all wrong, you can step back and gain some clarity. I see so many people pushing to move forward. Often, stepping back and thinking things through—understanding *why*—will tell you if you're setting the right goal.

I wanted to help people, so I set a goal to write *Get Out of Neutral*, my first book. I never stepped back and thought about why I was writing it. If I had, I would have seen what I really wanted was the residual income I could earn from royalties. Similarly, I never looked closely at why I wanted to be a motivational speaker. If I had, I would have seen I wanted the authority and celebrity a well-known speaker acquires. As my book failed, and I realized that the speaker's life was not for me, I had no choice but to stop what I was doing, step back, and take a closer look at my goals.

This was a turning point. I lost my house, and I lost some status in the community. Ultimately it was the best thing that could have happened: It allowed me to find the real goals that would align my life with my values and mission. I was able to move out of the lower levels of consciousness and into the Observer. That brought me clarity.

Ultimately, those few steps back resulted in about ten big steps forward. I went from obsessing about becoming an author and speaker to focusing on building residual income. That's when I started MorningCoach, realizing that freedom, my number one value, was also a major goal. It called for a different way of thinking. I wanted to be at home in my office—I call it my cave—not on the road traveling all the time and working for someone else.

My failure to evaluate my *whys* was painful for my family and myself, but it opened me up to what I needed to do. The best part of all is my original dream of being an author stayed alive, but as I approached it with more clarity, I was able to see that it wasn't fame I wanted; it was the income from royalties on the books and related products and the ability to help others.

What happened to me is an example of why it is so important to slow down and see goal setting as a process. Then you can let it work for you, without insisting on instantaneous results.

Writing down your goals and assessing the *why* of them is an ongoing exercise. Normally it is not completed in one sitting. Ideas will come to you as you're doing other things, and you will want to jot them down. That's why keeping a journal is so helpful in this process.

If you are having trouble setting goals, just focus on your next experience for now. What do you want to experience next in life? Write that down along with some steps to get there. You can build from there.

A Commitment to Excellence

We have just moved into a new house on Dawn Avenue in La Porte, Indiana, and life couldn't be better. Ronald Reagan is president, the 1980s are just getting started, and the Oakland Raiders, my Raiders, are a dynasty team and Super Bowl champions.

At age 11, I absolutely love the surprise of receiving mail. Running out to the mailbox, especially on a nice summer day, is something I look forward to every day. Today, as I take the mail out of the box, I can't believe my eyes. There's a letter addressed to me—and it's from Raiders headquarters! I'm so excited I can hardly breathe.

A few weeks earlier, I had written a letter to Al Davis, the owner of my beloved football team, to tell him how important the Oakland Raiders are to me. I love everything about them. They have the best uniforms—silver and black. They have all the outcasts that other teams don't want. They are a band of outlaws, rebels, bad guys—and I love them. I know every player and his history. I have Raiders clothes, sheets, lamps, and *Sports Illustrated* covers. My room looks like a Raiders shrine. I may be the only fan in my town, but I am the ultimate Raiders fan.

I run back to the house and drop down on the 1970s shag carpet in our living room to tear open the envelope. Out drops a media guide, along with a handwritten letter from Al Davis himself, telling me how great it is to have fans like me. He even says that if I ever have a chance to visit Oakland, he would love to meet me. I am in heaven—total cloud nine.

It is hard to imagine how one person could affect so many people, but you would not be reading this book if it weren't for Al Davis. His goals, his mission, and his values shaped me at an early age. He had two mottos that both meant so much to me. One was "Commitment to excellence" and the other was "Just win, baby." I took both of those notions to heart.

Davis rose through the ranks of football to not only dominate as an NFL owner but also to help build the NFL into the league it is today. I know you may be wondering why I am discussing his influence on me in a chapter on goals. There are a couple of reasons. The first is that he changed the way I look at life. The second is that the impact he had on me carries through to the thousands of people I affect today. Thinking about Davis makes me realize how much our goals and actions influence the people around us in ways we may not even realize. Those ripples may touch thousands, even millions, of people.

Davis went out to conquer on the football field, not thinking that he would change the world. He threw his passion into making his organization one of the best in the country, setting some amazing goals and accomplishing them. He built a community and a culture. And while he was doing that, his vision and leadership, his way of life, were on display for millions to see. I was one of those millions. At that early age, I became committed to my goals by seeing Davis manifest his.

When you are setting goals, remember that there is more at stake than just reaching your goals. You are making a statement about leadership, as well. You are a light for others to see. I know that Davis had some tough times in his older years. Toward the end of his career the Raiders declined, and he couldn't find the magic as the game changed. Even in those times, I continued to learn from him. I saw him struggle to hold on, and I saw when he realized that it was time to let go and focus on something else. That is what the Sacred Six is about.

The Sacred Six process isn't about only yourself. As you achieve your goals, you will become a guiding light for others, just as Davis was for me. Always remember the impact your decisions and behavior may have. As you apply the principles in this book, others are going to see what you are doing and take action based on your example.

I'm often asked how I get people to understand goal setting and the importance of staying positive. My answer? Lead by example. When people who are feeling negative about life see you succeeding, they will want to know how you're doing it.

The Day I Quit

I have talked about my excitement at going to the Florida Speakers Association meeting and getting support for my goal of becoming a motivational speaker, only to have that dream shot down by my roommate, Ed, when he said, "Who would listen to you anyway?"

Ed was a great friend who really cared about me, and I believe he genuinely thought he had my best interests at heart. He didn't want to see me disappointed. The truth about goals is that sometimes you *will* be disappointed. That is part of the growing process. Still, my advice is to be careful who you tell about your goals. Even the most well-intentioned people may try to talk you out of your dreams.

We never know how our goals may affect others. I do know that if you go out and succeed at what you really want to do, the world will be a better place for it. So don't let other people get in your way. Make sure that your goals are *your* goals, not what anyone else thinks they should be. Don't worry if someone tells you that you will never reach them. Keep your focus on the Sacred Six process and work at it every day.

Next, in Part II, you will learn how to take your goals and break them down into projects and daily tasks that will keep you moving forward in the direction of your dreams.

PART

INTO ACTION

CHAPTER

THE SACRED SIX GOAL PROJECTS

I can feel another awesome morning starting as I put pen to paper to write my to-do list. There is nothing quite like the feel of a Montblanc gliding across a blank sheet of paper. I think about all the things I have to do today for the business and for my family:

1. Meet with the sales team.
2. Finish reports.
3. Read e-mails from corporate.
4. Finish the allocation sheet.
5. Check on production status.
6. . . .

Oh, boy. I push my chair back from my desk and exhale. As I take a sip of tea, I'm starting to feel depressed. I had such high hopes for this week, and instead I'm feeling frustrated and overwhelmed. I know that at times like this I need to change my attitude, so I get up and go for a walk around the office, saying good morning to everyone I see. Inside, I still feel as if I'm drowning.

Upstairs there is an old storage area where no one ever goes, so I head there to find some peace. The room has a broken door, an old steel desk, a rickety chair, and three large file cabinets that are open wide, with papers spilling out in every direction—mass disorganization. I plop into the chair and look around, feeling as beat-up as those file cabinets. Another week has gone by, and I have a to-do list as long as a child's Christmas wish list. Why is my life like this? This is not what I planned.

I give myself a pep talk and think about my dream of writing a book. I am talking myself into it: I *can* live this dream. I have no idea where I will find the time, but I am going to work hard to develop the right mental attitude. I start to feel a little more positive, so I go downstairs and head back to my desk. I sit down, grab my pen, and continue writing down all the things I have to do. The list is ugly, that's for sure, but I just keep thinking, *I will get this done.*

That was a typical Monday for me before I discovered the Sacred Six process. In fact, I was feeling overwhelmed like that every single day. I think back to those chaotic times and breathe a sigh of relief because of what the Sacred Six has brought me. Do I still have chaos in my life? I guess you could call it that, but to me it is *organized* chaos.

The guts of the Sacred Six process are about organizing your goals into projects to work on and then breaking down those projects into manageable daily chunks so you will remain continually productive, not feeling as if you're drowning.

Back in the day, my to-do lists ran to more than 100 items, and when I compare my life then with where I am today, I realize I actually get much more done now. I love my new Mondays. My typical Monday goes like this: I get up, drink a glass of lemon water, and then make myself a cup of chai tea. I sit down at my desk and glance at my mission, review my values, and look over my goals. I then prioritize my week according to my Sacred Six projects. I know exactly what I am going to do and how long it will take. I check for any hair-on-fire moments (those surprises that pop up once in a while). Then I get to work.

I record my podcast and shoot a video for one of the courses on MorningCoach.com. Then I write 1,500 to 2,000 words for a magazine article or my blog or another of the books I'm working on, which include a fantasy novel series. Then I jog five miles, drink a smoothie, and I'm done by 9:30 A.M. Since I wake up around 6:30 A.M., my workday is about three hours long, and I'm committed to cutting that down. In those three hours I get more done than I did in a week in my old confused world. So what's the secret?

Time Poverty

Before the Sacred Six, I never really understood the importance of time. I thought that money was the most important thing in life. I have since learned that although money is important and necessary, the one thing we cannot get more of is time. I see so many people living in poverty—not of the financial kind, but of time.

It is one thing to have a bunch of great goals; it is another to have the time to actually accomplish them. An important part of the Sacred Six process is taking back your time, which equates to taking back your life. You have to recognize time as a commodity. You are either investing in it to create freedom or you are wasting it, which is a form of bondage.

In my corporate days, I lived for the weekend. I would rush through the week just to get past it. If you really think about it, this is a very sad situation. On five days out of seven I did not enjoy living. I was just wasting time. One of my major realizations came when I understood that tomorrow is not promised, so I have to make the most of today. That's when I made freedom one of my top values and went to work.

Of course, a realization like that doesn't change your life right away. While I was still working for someone else, I gave it my best, respecting that the time I was trading for money was important to my employer. I also recognized that I had to find ways to get my time back to do what I loved. That was critical to me. I went to work structuring my mission, values, and goals around that idea.

I think what most people really want to do is similar to what I have learned to do using the Sacred Six process. Given the choice between a work week of 60 hours with only 20 hours for family and hobbies, or a work week of 20 hours with 60 hours for family and fun—while still earning a living—who wouldn't choose the latter without hesitation?

In Search of Perfection

One of the most valuable things you can do is gain control of your productivity. There is a principle in economics called the Pareto principle, also known as the 80/20 rule or the law of the vital few. In 1906, Italian economist Vilfredo Pareto published a paper in which he observed that 80 percent of the land in Italy was owned by 20 percent of its people. He then derived the principle by looking in his garden, where 20 percent of the pea pods contained 80 percent of the peas. The Pareto principle is widely applied in business as a reminder to invest your time and energy where you can expect the greatest return. For example, Microsoft believes that if they fix the top 20 percent of reported bugs, then 80 percent of related errors in the system will automatically be fixed. When I first learned of the Pareto principle, I wanted to figure out how I could apply it in my life. If this law of the vital few was working in so many areas, how could it help me?

I started by looking at my list of projects at work and in my personal life. I then analyzed them all to see what was really working. As I dug deeper, I could see the Pareto principle at work. Literally 20 percent of my projects had yielded 80 percent of my results. If I could focus on the top 20 percent, why did I need the other 80 percent? This was an epiphany for me. Growing up, I had learned to strive for perfection in everything I did. If I focused on perfecting everything, yet only 20 percent of what I did generated the greatest return, wasn't I wasting a lot of effort?

When I thought about this wasted effort, I started noticing that most people focus a lot on the last phase of a project, on perfecting all the little details at the end. This is what keeps us from being done. So I realized that focusing on perfection was holding me back in a number of ways. I didn't need to be perfect; I needed to be finished. As the old saying goes, *Perfection is the opposite of done.*

This is why I can be done working for the day by 9:30 in the morning, and then go play golf, run to the beach, or spend time with my family. I understand the power of the Pareto principle, and I am always homing in on that 20 percent that brings me 80 percent of the returns and eliminating other tasks that are just wasted effort.

I know this is a challenge for most people; they want to do as much as they can, and they want to do it perfectly. This is holding you back from your dreams. You have to learn how to analyze what you are going after and how you are going to get there. Monitoring your activities like this takes only a few minutes a day, but it can add up to thousands of hours over a lifetime. What is important is not how much you get done but the effectiveness of what you do. A desire for perfection and a need to be busy are among the main reasons why people today have so much stress and anxiety. And that stress and anxiety is holding you back.

There is a big difference between being busy and working effectively.

Living in an Age of Distractions

My life before the Sacred Six: stacks of papers are piled on my desk. I look at one of them and move it to the opposite side of the desk. I take the books off my desk and put them on the shelf in the closet. My office is looking cleaner. Then I think, *I really need to clean the Jeep, inside and out.* I decide to pull the Jeep out of the garage and get to work on it.

As I am taking everything out of the Jeep, I notice that the shelves of the garage need to be organized. I clean the Jeep and then start tackling the shelves. I look outside and it is getting dark. *What time is it, anyway?* I glance at my watch. It is 7:30 P.M., and I have not yet written my blog. I run into the house, tired and mentally beat. I post on Facebook how tough a day it has been and that I'm so busy I can't get anything done.

I finish the blog and leave the office at 8:30 P.M. to get something to eat. I think to myself, *Where did the day go?* Time flies. I was superbusy today. I did so much yet accomplished so little.

Do you ever feel as if you are so busy that you can't get anything done? This is the busy disease, and we all have it to some degree. You think you are accomplishing things when you are just filling time with busywork. Remember when you were in grade school and the teacher would hand out photocopied sheets of math problems, then leave the room? That was busywork. Just something to keep us occupied as time passed.

Busywork is one of the great time stealers. Cleaning the car, cleaning the house, organizing the closet, and so on. You can't afford to let these things get in your way. If you can, pay someone else to do stuff like that for you. If you can't, realize that these tasks are not your top priorities. Does it really matter if your car is a bit dirty while you're working to achieve your dreams? No, it doesn't. You need to spend time on activities that are going to be productive for you. Don't let busyness steal your time and life.

Focus on the project that's pointing toward your goals and don't be distracted by nonessential tasks.

A lot of stress and anxiety is caused by not doing something we should be doing, but just as much is caused by doing something that is distracting us from what's important. It is amazing how tired you become when this occurs.

I remember being at work with nothing to do, so I played busy—acted as though I was working on the computer, picking up the phone and making calls, even walking around the office. I was so tired on those days—dead tired compared with the days when I actually did some real work.

This is the problem with just going through the motions day in and day out: It is not just a time stealer but an energy stealer, as well. It is as if the Universe (God) knows you have been messing around, so you pay the price with exhaustion. Don't let this be you. Focus on activities that are going to take you to your dreams. You deserve better than to waste valuable currency, which is running out even as I type this . . .

The Power of *No*

One of the most valuable words in the English language is *no*. Learning how to use it can be a powerful tool. When you feel the urge to clean the garage in order to avoid the task at hand, just say no. If someone asks you to do something you don't want to do, just say no. If you are going to stay focused and on task, you must learn to exercise your *no* muscle.

No is a powerful word, and one that is not used enough. Once you have your plan in place, it is all about execution. If you are too busy working on needless tasks, you will never be able to execute. In order to execute, you have to be free and clear to focus. This is why letting go of time-wasting activities is so important.

One thing that has helped me say no is being able to access peace. This is critical for avoiding stress and anxiety. I know that slowing down can be particularly challenging for a type A, driven sort, but Finding Peace techniques can make a huge difference in your life.

Finding Peace

Cleansing Breath

Breathing techniques work well for releasing stress and anxiety so you can restore your focus. One of my favorite techniques for letting things go and finding peace is the cleansing breath. If someone asks me to do something I don't have time to do, I relax, say no, and then take a cleansing breath.

To take a cleansing breath, simply stop and inhale deeply, filling your lungs with air down to your abdomen. Then slowly release the air through your mouth.

I do this on the golf course before taking a swing. I focus on releasing all the energy of stress, letting the breath take away any tension as I exhale.

The Rubber Band

Another effective tool for finding peace is a simple rubber band. It has multiple uses. One is to put it around your wrist and snap it when you start to think negative thoughts. Once you've done this for a while, just looking at

---

the rubber band will help you stay positive. Another use for the rubber band is to snap it when you lose focus.

I always have a rubber band on my wrist to help me stay positive and focused. In fact, I had a MorningCoach bracelet imprinted with the message *Always Positive* made especially for this purpose.

Becoming Present

This last technique can be used anytime you want to get centered. It works by helping you move out of psychological time and focus on the present moment.

Take any object on your desk, like a pen or a pencil, and look at it deeply. This means noticing even the smallest details, like the manufacturer's name printed on the side or the gradations of color.

Once you have looked intently at the object for a few seconds, raise your eyes and look around the room. Look at the objects in the room and focus on being fully present. Let go of anything else in your mind and just focus on where you are and what is around you.

This technique will help you stay in the here and now, so that your mind doesn't get too far ahead of you. It can also help you feel less overwhelmed. *Now* is the only time we truly have, so be in the moment and feel peace.

Breaking Goals into Projects

Now that you understand how important it is to focus and stay on task, you need a game plan for taking the goals you set and making them happen. Once you have set your goals, take the top six goals you want to hit and check to make sure they are aligned with your mission and values.

If any goal doesn't pass the test, replace it with another goal from your master list. If your goals are not aligned with your mission and values, you will be like a car with its wheels out of alignment—wobbling all over the place and unable to move forward in a straight line.

Once you have chosen the six goals that are aligned with your values and will take you to your mission, you need to break them into smaller goals, or *projects*. Each goal will have projects that need to be completed in order to reach it.

For example, let's take the goal of starting an online blog. This is in alignment with a mission of making the world a better place and creating a business that builds on a passion and requires only a few hours of work per week. Okay, yes, this was one of my goals, but let's say it's one you share. You first need to consider what projects must be completed in order to get your blog up and running. Your project list might look something like this:

1. Choose a blogging platform.
    A blogging platform, or "content management system," is the service or software that allows you to post blogs. Among the most popular free blogging platforms are WordPress, Blogger, Tumblr, Squarespace, and Google+, but to find the one that's best for your purposes, you could view online videos or do a web search.

2. Design your logo and blog site.
    Many of the most popular blogging platforms have templates you can use to design your blog, or you could hire a professional designer, as I did.

3. Select a web-hosting service.

   It is also necessary to select a service to host your blog. The web-hosting service provides the server on which your blog is stored.

4. Write an "About" page.

   This is where you describe the subject of the blog, as well as say something about yourself and why you are blogging.

5. Write the first blog post.

   Blog posts generally run from 500 to 750 words. You might also want to include images.

From here, there are a number of projects you could add to the list, such as hiring an editor to polish the text before putting your ideas out to the world. To make people aware of your blog, you could include links to Facebook, Twitter, Instagram, and other social media, and come up with other avenues of promotion, online and offline. If you want to earn money with your blog, you could solicit advertising or offer products for sale.

Some of these projects can be worked on simultaneously, such as planning promotions while the blog is being edited, whereas others, such as selecting a blogging platform and web-hosting service, will need to be finished before moving on to the next project.

Whatever your goal, it will have its own set of projects. To give you another example, we can look at a personal goal I'm working on now: lowering my golf handicap to a single digit. My projects for this goal are:

1. Find a coach and set up lessons.

2. Set up a weekly practice schedule—putting, chipping, long irons, short irons, woods.

3. Play a round of golf three to four times a week.

4. Subscribe to *Golf Digest* and *Golf* magazine— and read them!

5. Record TV shows on the Golf Channel and schedule times to view them.

Some of these projects are one-shots that can be completed quickly—finding a coach and scheduling lessons, for example. Others will require ongoing or daily activities. What's important is that I have a plan to get it all done and hit my goal.

The two goals I have just laid out—creating a blog and lowering my golf handicap—will yield a total of ten or more projects to work on. This is where the process gets tough. If you have 100 goals on your master list, you can imagine how many projects you would have to work on to hit your targets. That's why you have to prioritize both your goals and your projects. You can't be working on everything at the same time. Remember, in projects, six is the magic number. Most of us cannot focus on more than six at one time.

Prioritizing Goals and Projects

Prioritization is one of the most important concepts in all aspects of the Sacred Six process. Not setting priorities is a major reason people fail to hit their goals. Jumping haphazardly from goal to goal rather than concentrating on a few select goals and following through can make you lose momentum. In fact, it can even create *reverse* momentum, so that you end up taking four steps back for every three steps forward, and never achieve what you set out to do. Sure, you can have as many goals as you want, but in order to achieve them you will need to prioritize them, so that you know what to work on first. Then, as you reach a goal, you can check if off your list and move on to the next.

To give you an idea how prioritization works, let's take a look at how Sarah, a working mom juggling multiple roles, has set up her goals and projects. Sarah is the CEO of her own company, which she started after giving up a 20-year corporate career. She has spent the past five years getting the company, which distributes computer equipment, to a place of profitability. She now has a team of 20 people, plus a network of suppliers. In addition to running her company, Sarah is raising two children, ages 8 and 11, and pursuing her passion for theater as an aspiring actress. If you look at everything she has going on, you might wonder how she is ever going to be able to live her dreams.

It all rests on the Sacred Six. Sarah has hit her career goal by becoming CEO of her company, but now she wants to grow the business. That is one of her mission goals. Another of her mission goals is to be an amazing mother. Sarah has two other goals: to be a great leader at work and to grow as an actress. Like many of us, her plate is full. So here's how she has prioritized her goals:

1. Support my children's growth by listening to them and helping them reach their potential.

2. Grow my company by double digits while creating systems that give me more free time to spend with family.

3. Act in a play this year.

4. Understand options trading in order to generate more income.

Sarah has made sure that her goals are aligned with her mission to be the best mother she can be while growing her business to ensure a safe and secure future for her family. She has also made sure they are aligned with her values: spirituality, family, health, adventure, and personal growth. Breaking her goals down into projects, she comes up with this list:

Goal 1: Support my children's growth by listening to them and helping them reach their potential.

☐ Project: Improve my listening skills and patience.

☐ Project: Understand nutrition and exercise.

☐ Project: Learn a second language to work on with the children.

Goal 2: Grow my company by double digits while creating systems that give me more free time to spend with family.

☐ Project: Work with sales and marketing to build goals in that division.

☐ Project: Focus on acquiring new companies and finding joint ventures.

☐ Project: Work with research and development to come up with new products.

Goal 3: Act in a play this year.

- ☐ Project: Take acting classes.
- ☐ Project: Join a theater group.

Goal 4: Understand options trading in order to generate more income.

- ☐ Project: Take an options trading class.
- ☐ Project: Open an options account.

These are only the top four of Sarah's goals, and already we can tell how much time and effort will be involved in reaching them. Once she has laid out the steps involved, Sarah can then prioritize her projects. Between the four goals on her list, Sarah has ten projects to choose from. She selects the six she will work on after considering which projects will most likely move her closer to her mission.

Sarah's Sacred Six projects list then looks like this:

1. Improve my listening skills and patience.
2. Work with sales and marketing to build goals.
3. Focus on company acquisitions skills.
4. Take an acting class.
5. Learn a second language.
6. Learn about options trading.

These six projects reflect what is most important to Sarah right now. She will have other work and family obligations to deal with, but for now she has a manageable plan to reach her goals and move toward her mission.

Prioritizing is something most people don't do. Instead they run around with no focused direction, putting out fires as they arise. The Sacred Six process counteracts that tendency to go off in all directions.

To see how two other people—Matthew, a stay-at-home dad, and Ricky, a salesman who wants to learn piano—prioritize their goals and projects, turn to Appendix II (page 175).

Changing Projects

Once you have drawn up your list of projects, the only way to cross a project off the list is to complete it—or to have a *very* good reason to drop it. The Sacred Six process is designed to support you in taking your projects all the way to completion, but sometimes something unexpected comes up, or you realize that a project is just never going to work, never going to take you to your goal, no matter what you do, so you will have to adjust your project list. That's not ideal, but it happens.

One reason for taking a project off your list is that it wasn't the right project in the first place. It's important not to chase after projects simply to find happiness. This is why I have emphasized moving into the Observer state when you are setting goals and projects. If you make decisions in the ego state, you will keep flitting from project to project, only to realize that you aren't happy no matter what you accomplish. (My Mastermind group [a group of people who get together to help you in business and life] calls that "chasing butterflies"—chasing every shiny object that comes your way and catching none because you are so distracted.) Don't decide, for example, to buy a new stove just because your sister raves about hers, when what you really need to do is buy a computer to write your blog or complete your course work. Before you put a project on your list *or* take one off, make sure you have considered your reasons from the Observer state. Your focus always should be on the projects that will move you toward your mission and goals.

Finding Your Own Sacred Six

Now it's your turn to put a plan in place so you can move toward your dreams. Most of us haven't been taught how to achieve our dreams. In fact, we are more often taught just the opposite—to stop dreaming and get down to work. Now is the time to build the life you desire and not wait for others to do it or for circumstances to dictate your future. Your next step is to engage fully with the Sacred Six and create goals and projects that are aligned with your mission and values.

To avoid chasing butterflies, identify your goals and projects from the standpoint of the Observer—your true self—and not from the ego. That way, your goals will reflect what you care about at the deepest level. To quiet the ego mind and move into the Observer state before setting goals and projects, you could do one of the exercises from Chapter 2—the Mirror Ritual (page 30) or Quiet the Mind (page 31)—or any other relaxation method that works for you.

Once you have connected with the Observer, take pen and paper or your journal and prepare to write out your list of goals and projects and then prioritize your action steps. Be sure to leave plenty of time for this. The more thought you give to your goals and projects, the more likely they will take you where you want to go. When you are ready, you can proceed with the following steps:

- Make a master list of *all* your goals, whether you have 2 or 10 or 100.

- Run down your list of goals and make sure they are all in alignment with your mission and values. Eliminate any goals that are not.

- Look at each goal carefully and reflect on *why* you want to achieve it. Make sure the goal is not ego driven.

- Prioritize your goals, picking the top five to ten.

- Take the top five to ten goals you have selected and list the projects you will need to complete in order to achieve those goals.

- Prioritize your list of projects, and then pick the top six. These are your Sacred Six projects.

It is important not to rush this part of the Sacred Six process. Often I make a Saturday activity of sitting down and taking a close look at my goals and the projects they will require, then spending time mapping out a game plan.

Once your Sacred Six projects are in place, the rest is a matter of execution. We now move on to one of the most powerful, life-changing steps in the Sacred Six process: setting up daily actions that will allow you to complete your projects and hit your goals.

CHAPTER
7

THE SACRED SIX DAILY TASKS

Saturday? I have to work on a Saturday? And we've just been through a hurricane. There have been horrendous storms over the past few days, the power is only just coming back on, and I'm getting called into the office to start making up for three days of missed work.

I drive to work, passing the businesses near the Miami airport that have closed—the Pan American Airlines offices, the jet engine repair shops, the old hotels. Miami used to be a mecca for aviation, but ever since Pan Am went out of business in 1991, the local industry has been dying a slow death. I'm feeling that way myself as I climb to the second floor of the dark, airless building that houses our main office.

Dejected, I go straight to my office to start my day. As I sit at my desk, thinking about all the things I need to do, the old Earl Nightingale motivation tapes spring to mind. I keep hearing Nightingale telling the story about the advice efficiency consultant Ivy Lee gave Charles Schwab. For some reason, it's playing over and over in my mind: Write down the top six things you need to do, prioritize them, then start working on the first one and move on to the second only when the first is done.

I sit back in my chair and let out a cleansing breath. Then I start to write out my list of six things I need to get done today. I find that it's not as easy as Lee made it sound. What about the things I need to pick up from the store? Where do they fit? How about household projects? Confused, I sit back and once again think, *There must be a better way.*

That's when I started to build out the Sacred Six process, realizing that it wasn't just the tasks Lee talked about that needed to be written down. Those tasks needed to be part of an entire plan that was spelled out clearly. That plan should help me move forward and make consistent progress. In Japanese, this concept is called *kaizen*, literally *change for the better*, and it was popular in the automotive industry in the 1980s and 1990s. Applying the philosophy of continuous improvement, the Toyota Corporation almost single-handedly transformed Japanese industry from makers of cheap electronics to manufacturers of the best cars on the market, dominating the auto industry at the time. That lesson had always stuck with me, and I realized I needed to apply it to my own situation. I needed to keep getting better, and I had to have a clear system for doing that.

That's when I started establishing my mission, values, and goals. It was only after I had those in place that it made sense to contemplate the activities required to get me where I wanted to go. That is where the projects and daily tasks came in. Just as I described in Chapter 6, I reviewed all my goals and built out projects, then prioritized the ones that were most important. I picked my top six projects, and then the lightbulb came on: I needed daily tasks to get those six projects done. These tasks became my *daily* Sacred Six.

This is where the real work lies, in the incremental steps you take every day to reach your goals and ultimately your mission. I did not write this chapter all at once, for example. It was the 1,000 to 2,000 words I wrote each day that got me to the end of the chapter. And it was working on those chapters consistently, day by day, that got the book written. That is how I accomplished my goal of writing a book, and in the same way, daily tasks are going to help you accomplish your goals.

So once you have your Sacred Six projects in place, your next step is to organize your life so you are moving toward your goals on a daily basis. Just as *the Sacred Six* refers to the projects that will move you closer to your goals, it also refers to the six daily tasks you are going to work on to help you complete your projects.

Sacred Tasks Versus Everyday Tasks

When I started to write down my Sacred Six daily tasks, I began feeling a little frustrated. Work and other commitments kept popping up. I had sales reports due, business travel coming up, and home issues to deal with. Feeling overwhelmed, I decided to just write down *everything* I had to do. With all these obligations, I noticed I was having trouble fitting in my dream to-dos. Then I recognized something important.

There are times when you are not going to be able to work on your six sacred tasks every day. You may have a family, a career, and all kinds of other commitments, which means you will have other daily tasks you need to do as well as your Sacred Six. The Sacred Six doesn't always have to be six tasks; it can be just two or even one if that's all you can handle that day. What is key is that whatever task you take on should be sacred—should be fully aligned with your life's purpose and moving you toward your dreams, and you should be doing it every day.

Right now, the two sacred daily tasks I do without fail are preparing my podcast and studying Spanish.

Dedicated Practice

When the Sacred Six process was in the formation stage, I was still at the job I hated. I was working 50 to 60 hours a week, so I had only so many hours left in the day to dedicate to my Sacred Six. My first Sacred Six goal was to write my first book, and I set a goal of finishing the writing within six months and getting the book printed so I could sell it. At the time my immediate reason for doing this was to break free from my job, but if I'm being honest I also thought the book would bring me riches and a luxurious lifestyle.

Since my goal was to finish my book in six months, that meant I needed to turn out 500 to 1,000 words every day. That led me to another project. I couldn't type back then, which made the writing process much harder and slower. So I added a new project to the goal of writing the book: learning to type. I bought the *Mavis Beacon Teaches Typing* tutorial software program and made learning to type one of my Sacred Six goals. I then had two items on my list of sacred tasks to do every day: Write 500 to 1,000 words and practice typing for 30 minutes.

When I added the project of learning to type, I decided I would go into work early and spend 30 minutes typing. I also looked for opportunities later in the day to practice, finding another 30 minutes here or there. I was focused on getting better every day, and it was amazing how much my typing improved in just a month. I wasn't about to enter any speed contests, but at least I could touch-type. It was the first time in my life that I had focused on a specific practice, and it was paying off for me in other ways, as well.

Dedicated practice is the foundation of the Sacred Six. It means staying with an activity until you improve or master it. A daily commitment to both writing and typing enabled me to achieve my goal of finishing the book. More importantly, it showed me the power of the daily sacred tasks.

Focus Management

A lot of ink has been spilled in recent years over how to manage your time. In fact, there are more books on time management than on almost all other areas of productivity combined. If you are focusing on time management, then break out that brick of a mobile phone you carried around back in the 1990s, because you are living in the past. It is time to understand the truth. Productivity is not about time management; it is all about focus.

Text messages, Facebook, Twitter, Skype, meetings, family, television, e-mail, the list goes on and on—we live in an age of distractions. If you are going to move toward your dreams, you have to get a handle on the distractions. Focusing is hard enough without all this input. When I'm on my MacBook Air, I shut down all notifications that pop up on the right side of the screen. As a matter of fact, when I write, I use a program called Scrivener which allows me to block out everything except what I'm working on. I do this as part of my focus-management plan.

As you start implementing the daily tasks that will take you toward your goals, it will be critically important to manage your focus. This means when you are working on a Sacred Six task, you are *not* allowed to text, check e-mail, take phone calls, give in to any interruptions, or do anything but the task at hand. There will be no multitasking during your Sacred Six activities.

I view distraction as a disease. I can't stand being in meetings with people who are glued to their phones or tablets. This really is an epidemic. People cannot get away from their electronic leashes. It's not that I'm anti-technology. I love my devices, and there are times when I, too, find myself attached to them. I just make a point of getting away from the distractions when I'm working on my daily tasks.

Admittedly, it wasn't long ago that I suffered from the virus . . .

I am pounding away on the keys, the words are flowing, and I am loving life, when I glance over at my other computer, and there is a message from Mom: *JB, check out this video.* So I turn away from my writing to click on the video link. It takes me to YouTube, and next thing I know, I'm watching some baby playing with a horse. I spend the next few minutes laughing at the baby and the horse. Then the video ends, and I see a barking cat in one of the videos on the YouTube sidebar. Well, I just have to see that.

The next thing I know, 30 minutes have flown by. I can't stop myself now. Since I am already distracted from my writing task, I decide to check my e-mail. And then there is Facebook. Next thing I know, it is four in the afternoon. I have to get back to my writing, or I'll never finish what I set out to do. So I turn on some music and turn back to my computer. At this point, I have no idea where I left off, so I have to reread half of what I wrote earlier. I'm totally off my game.

This is how easily an innocent little break can turn into a daily game of distraction. One thing leads to another. These small lapses in focus are killing our dreams. It is not the big things like family emergencies or medical crises that are getting in our way, and that is why time management is so passé. It is not about how much time you have blocked off; it is about what you are actually focused on during that time.

Focus management is what enables me to do two podcasts, write 2,000 words, work out, and be done for the day by 9:30 A.M. I am totally focused on the task at hand. My formula for this is very simple: Focus in 50-minute chunks. That way, if something important does come to my attention, I can handle it. I work for 50 minutes, take a 10-minute break for distractions, and then get back to the task.

Think about it like this: If you have eight hours in a workday, and you are working on six main projects daily, and you work in 50-minute chunks with 10 minutes in between, that means you will spend about five hours on your Sacred Six, plus 50 minutes for distractions, leaving you two free hours to work on something else. Ultimately you want your daily Sacred Six to work like this. Start on the first task, work on it for 50 minutes, and finish it. Then take a ten-minute break. Come back and start on task number two. It's that simple. Just keep the flow going.

I know you may be thinking, *What if a task takes longer than 50 minutes?* If a task runs well past 50 minutes, then you probably should have broken it down into two tasks. I admit this can be a challenge sometimes, so don't get stuck trying to be perfect at this. Do your best to complete each task in 50 minutes, and don't stress if it runs longer. Just adjust. The same task may take less time one day and more the next. You will need to be flexible. The most important thing is to work on your Sacred Six only when your mind is focused. You will probably find that your focus diminishes after about 50 minutes.

Putting on Blinders

I have an exercise that really helps me stay focused. It is inspired by the way horses behave. When a racehorse is easily distracted by other horses and the crowds at the track, his trainer will put blinders on him. The blinders close off the horse's peripheral vision so he stays focused on the course ahead. A focused horse performs better. So does a focused person.

When I need to focus and get to work, I put on blinders. I raise my hands to my face, place one hand on each side of my head, with the thumbs next to my ears and the fingers pointing straight forward so they block my peripheral vision. Then I silently say to myself, "Focus." This little trick moves my mind to a more concentrated state. The awesome thing is that the more you do this exercise, the easier it becomes to trigger your mind to focus on the task at hand.

Breaking Projects into Daily Tasks

The Sacred Six process is all about making forward progress on a daily basis. The idea is to just keep rowing the boat and eventually you will get to the other side. To do that, you have to know what tasks you need to be working on each day.

You have already set your goals and started breaking them into projects to complete those goals. You have prioritized those projects so you know which ones are most important. Now you need to take your projects and put daily tasks to them. This means more prioritization. Remember, the most common reason people fail to reach their goals is that they have too many irons in the fire. Prioritizing your tasks solves that.

If you have a job or family responsibilities, you may only have time to work on one or two sacred tasks each day, but you may have a list of dozens and dozens of tasks that need to get done. You can see how this could become an issue. I have seen to-do lists with more than 100 items on them. How could anyone possibly get all that done? Talk about distracting, not to mention the mental stress of just looking at a list like that! It's better to do a few great things each day than to do a lot of ineffective things.

The judgments you make in prioritizing are crucial to your productivity. That is why the first steps in the Sacred Six process were about gaining clarity through alignment of your mission, values, and goals. That is really the only way to make sure you are prioritizing properly.

What you need to do now is look at the projects you prioritized in Chapter 6. You should have no more than six on that list. Now you will take each project and break it down into daily tasks.

Think of Sarah, whose process I described in Chapter 6. Her goals are to grow her company and build her relationships with her children, and she has six projects to work on to take her toward those goals. As CEO of her company, Sarah has huge responsibilities on a daily basis. Plus she's a mom, so she has only a few hours a day to work on her Sacred Six tasks. What's good is that some of her projects are work related, so the daily tasks involved will fit easily into her workday. She has prioritized those projects, as well as some projects related to building her relationship with her children.

Looking at Sarah's projects, what are some daily tasks that would move her toward them?

1. Develop listening skills and patience.

Listening is a skill that can be learned, so Sarah's first task is to buy or borrow three books on listening skills. Once she has the books, she can strike that task from her list and replace it with scheduling 30 minutes daily to read the books.

To practice patience, Sarah can use the rubber band technique on page 101 in a slightly different way. She will wear the rubber band around her wrist and flick it whenever she becomes aware that she is losing patience.

2. Work with sales and marketing to build out goals.

This is a work-related project. Among the daily tasks Sarah could put in place would be to dedicate one hour to the sales and marketing team during which she reviews with the group what is needed and sets new goals focused on sales growth. Once she decides she has enough forward momentum on this project, she can move on to another one.

The Sacred Six process enables you to measure over time how efficient and skilled you have become. You will be able to add skills much more rapidly, which will have a domino effect in your life, taking you much faster toward your dreams. Sarah can probably complete tasks 1 and 2 within two to three months.

3. Work on acquiring new companies and finding joint ventures.

This is another work-related task that Sarah can easily fit into her day. She has to allocate only 30 to 60 minutes to this. She will meet with her acquisitions team every day and focus on ways the company can improve in this area. This task will probably be ongoing as Sarah grows the company.

4. Take an acting class.

To work toward her goal of acting in a play this year, Sarah chose taking an acting class as a priority project. This does not necessarily warrant a daily activity, though if she wants to be a great actress, I believe that daily practice is essential. Sarah might decide to do some acting exercises daily and then take an acting class once a week. That way she will make consistent progress toward improving her skill.

5. Learn a second language.

This is another project Sarah prioritized for her goal of helping her children. There are several daily tasks she could do. She could listen to language MP3s in the car on the way to work. She could also take a class during the week and follow up with an hour of study every day. There are a number of ways to learn a second language, but practice and immersion are critical, so Sarah has to commit to working on it daily. If she stops for even a few days, she will likely take some steps backward. She needs to keep this project on her list until she is fluent.

6. Learn about options trading.

This project could be completed with a few weekend classes and some practice periods in between. Or Sarah could sign up for an online class and study every day for 15 to 30 minutes. She will probably need to continue this task for a few months before she is ready to replace it.

Sarah now has a game plan for achieving her goals. Some tasks will take longer than others, but the Sacred Six process is flexible, moving at the pace you choose.

A Project-Management System

If you look at Sarah's projects and tasks, you will see that some are related to her mission of helping her family, whereas others are related to her work. The Sacred Six process works for all goals, whether mission goals, family or personal goals, work goals, or stretch goals.

Whatever kind of project you are working on, the principles and steps remain the same. The one caveat is that there may be times when you need to complete a project that is *not* a Sacred Six project—not in alignment with your mission and values. It's just an obligation from your job or personal life. If this is the case, then you can work through those projects and tasks in the same way you would work through a project for your own goals; just don't worry about looking for alignment with your mission and values. Go right to the projects, prioritize them, and break them down into daily tasks. This process is a great way to get anything done. It sharpens your focus and eliminates distractions.

Let's take a closer look at what Sarah's day will look like once she is organized. She gets up and heads to the gym. She returns home and gets herself and her family ready for the day. She jumps in the car, pushes play on the media player, and her language-learning tapes start up. She drops off the children at school and then heads to work, continuing to learn her second language as she drives.

Sarah gets to work and immediately plans her day using the Sacred Six process, focusing on the tasks she will do and in what order. She then works her way through the day, holding meetings with acquisitions and sales at which she is fully focused, then spending 30 minutes at lunch reading about options or taking an online options course. At the end of her workday, she gets in the car and again pushes play on the media player, resuming her language lesson. While waiting to pick up her children, Sarah texts the acting school and schedules a class. At home she spends quality time with her children, focusing on being patient with them. After dinner, she practices a scene for acting class and runs lines with her husband. She then takes a breather and watches her favorite TV show. Heading to bed, she grabs her book on listening and reads until she falls asleep.

That is Sarah in full Sacred Six process mode. If it helps her stay disciplined, she can carry her priority list with her in her purse or on her phone and check off items as she completes them. The Sacred Six process is a way for your entire life to work more efficiently and for you to stay focused on the things you need to do every day to pursue your dreams.

Now It's Your Turn

At first, all these steps may seem a bit complicated, but once you immerse yourself in the process, you will find that it is easy to organize yourself and see the progress you are making. That said, I would caution you not to get *too* caught up in the planning and organization. The goal, after all, is to take action. There is no point in spending a lot of time putting your plan down on paper if you are not going to execute the plan. The Sacred Six requires daily action to make progress toward your life goals.

Think of the Sacred Six as a lifestyle and a method of self-care. It is a process of organization that can help you become more effective in your career and your relationships. And it will help you find inner peace because you will know that you are on the right path at all times. The Sacred Six also works metaphysically, because as you become more organized, you will create an energetic alignment with your higher source—Universe (God)—which leads to peace, happiness, and joy.

It takes time to create the habit of working on your Sacred Six every day. My advice is simply to keep following the process until it becomes second nature. If at any point you get stuck, remember that motivation comes from the *why*s in your life. It will come as you continually review your mission, making sure that it is aligned with your values and goals. The key to this process is to get into an action habit. As items come off the list and you see progress, it will create more forward momentum.

The whole Sacred Six process is about keeping your focus. Just as you will do no more than six projects at a time, you will take on no more than six daily tasks at a time. As you finish one task, you can replace it with another.

Don't forget to review your mission, values, and goals, and make sure they are all in alignment. Then take a look at the projects you prioritized in Chapter 6, breaking them down into daily tasks so you will know exactly what you need to be working on every day. This will take some effort and time, but your life is too important to leave it to chance. The process will get easier as you make it a habitual part of your life.

A Note about Weekends

As you start writing down the six things you are going to start doing today (or tomorrow, if you are writing your daily task list at night), you may be wondering what to do about weekends. Are you meant to be working on your daily tasks seven days a week?

People ask me this a lot, and it can be a tough question to answer. There are certain tasks you need to do every day, even on the weekends. Learning a language is one example. You will go much further much faster if you keep up with it seven days a week. Similarly, if you are trying to establish a keystone habit of getting up early, then it will be easier to make that part of your routine if you set your alarm for the same time every day, including Saturday and Sunday. You have to decide all this for yourself.

In general, I suggest that if you are working toward a behavioral change, then it's best to continue it through the weekend. If it's an organizational or a business task, like learning about options trading, then you can take the weekends off. I only do MorningCoach podcasts Monday through Friday, but when I wanted to improve my golf game, I worked on it every day.

Creating Your Sacred Six Daily Plan

Success follows imperfect action. Hold that thought in your mind as you draw up your Sacred Six daily plan. If you are like me, you want everything to fit neatly into boxes, but that is not the way the world works. You will have curveballs thrown at you every day. Just keep your focus on the task at hand. Even a little focus management will take you far. Most people have no more than a to-do list to organize their time and have never even considered this sort of daily schedule. However, it is key to the success of the Sacred Six process.

Since the Sacred Six is a dynamic process, as you change, you will need to make continual adjustments. I recommend reviewing your daily tasks every weekday. Go through the list and review your game plan for the day. Depending on your mission you may need to do this review on the weekend as well as during the week. This would apply, for example, to a musician who plays gigs on the weekend.

Any significant life change will call for a review of the entire process, but I like to review specific aspects of the Sacred Six on the following schedule:

- **Mission:** Review annually.

- **Values:** Review bi-annually.

- **Goals:** Review quarterly.

- **Projects:** Review monthly, or as one is completed.

Moving Forward

At this point you may be feeling as if the Sacred Six process involves too much work, but I want to stress *this is your life.* Do you truly want to live your dreams? Has what you've been doing up until now gotten you there? If not, then you need to do something drastically different, and you need to do it now. The Sacred Six can get you where you want to go, but you have to put in the effort—take the action, keep at it, and have faith. As the Quakers say, "Pray with your feet moving."

So now that you have your daily task list, you can look at support tools that will keep you moving forward.

CHAPTER
8

SUPPORTING YOUR SACRED SIX

Filled with sleepy thoughts and positive dreams, I awaken to my dog, Niko, staring at me to get up and serve him breakfast. I look over at the clock on my iPad Mini; the bright blue letters shine 6:35 A.M. I rise, pat Niko on the head, and let him know he has another hour before I can feed him. I walk into my closet and grab my robe before heading downstairs with Niko trailing right behind. His yellow Lab energy is giving me what I need this morning.

It's a beautiful Florida morning. I head into the kitchen; down my morning cocktail of lemon juice, chia seeds, and water; and then brew some chamomile tea. Once my tea is ready, I take it to my office, sit down at my desk, and look over my mission. I then review my goals, so that I have the motivation I need to take on the day. Next I look at my Sacred Six daily tasks. I have two podcasts to produce, 2,000 words to write for my book, and one blog post due today. Those are my main activities. I also have to work on my golf game and study some spiritual texts. After organizing my Sacred Six, I get to work. I pull out my folder and outline my two podcasts.

As I sip my tea, I open my computer, hit the record button, and off I go.

One podcast done, then the next. I look at the clock; it is 7:15 A.M. and time to feed Niko. This is not part of my Sacred Six, but if I don't do it, I won't get any more of my tasks done. After feeding Niko and letting him out, I open the writing program on my computer and pound out 2,000 words. I look at the clock, and it is nearly 8:30 A.M. At this point, I am pretty much done with my main activities for the day, so I go for a five-mile run. By the time I have finished my run and showered, it's not quite 9:30 A.M. I have the rest of the day to work on my golf game and read some spiritual texts. I spend the next 20 minutes journaling my thoughts on life. Among the things I write about is how great it feels to accomplish so much, all before most people have even started their day.

I get a lot of questions from people wanting to know if life has always worked this way for me. By now you know that I would be lying if I said yes. It took me a long time to figure out what is important to me and then to organize my life around it. As I have communicated throughout this book, the Sacred Six is a lifestyle, and it took a while for that lifestyle to take hold. Once it did, however, I was amazed at how much my life changed. I finally had the energy, peace of mind, and confidence to go after the

132

things I had always dreamed of. After completing the exercises in the preceding chapters, you, too, have what you need to start living the lifestyle.

TOOLS TO SUPPORT YOUR DAILY PRACTICE

Once the Sacred Six process is working for you, it will take on a momentum of its own. It just requires some buy-in on your part, as well as behavioral changes. Now that you have the fundamentals in place—your mission, values, goals, projects, and daily tasks—there are a number of tools to help you organize the process and maximize its effects. The five key tools, I have found, are a to-do list, notes, a calendar, a journal, and a customer relationship management system (CRM).

Each of these has a particular function in the process and will play a foundational role in getting the ball rolling for you. There are probably hundreds of ways to employ each tool; you will need to find the way that works best for you and is the most enjoyable. It is important that you avoid associating the Sacred Six process with pain. You need to have fun with it or you will most likely quit.

It's a bit like going to the gym. If you drive yourself through your workout until you feel pain, eventually your body and your brain will shut down, and you will avoid the gym altogether. In contrast, I run every morning because I *love* running. I keep doing it day after day because it energizes me and makes me feel good. Sure, there is work involved in running and sometimes it's hard, but both my body and brain are primed to stay with it. You want to look for ways to enjoy the daily aspects of the Sacred Six process to keep you motivated and on the right track. The payoff is to see results.

To-Do List

Let's tackle to-do lists first since you are probably familiar with them and you will be working with them day in and day out. There are a number of software programs you can use to help you keep track of your to-dos. Just jump onto glossinger.com for all the latest techniques and technology that will help you with the Sacred Six process. The bottom line is you should use whatever form feels best to you. If you use a software program, make sure it is easy to use. It should also be mobile so you can take it with you and access it on the go.

I wrote out my original to-do lists longhand in a notebook, and that's an option if you aren't technologically inclined. There are still times when I love to write my Sacred Six down on actual paper with an actual pen. I love using a leather-bound notebook because it's a beautiful object that makes me want to write in it. Sometimes the tactile feel of pen on paper has real benefits. Psychologists and neurologists have found there is a cognitive payoff to writing longhand. It improves attention, memory, and manual dexterity, developing the brain in ways that are similar to the benefits you would get from learning a musical instrument.

I like to organize my goals and projects in one sitting every three months and then monitor my goal projects monthly. From there, I create my list of daily tasks that need to get done to complete my goal projects, writing them down and prioritizing them. Typically I sketch out the list on a yellow pad first because I like to keep my notebook neat and sacred. However, I know a lot of people who like to use one notebook to write down everything. You should do what works best for you. Once I have my prioritized list of daily tasks, I transfer it to my notebook and take action on the tasks. Every morning when I look at my mission and goals and review my projects and daily tasks, I add to the daily list anything I didn't get done the day before or anything new I need to do. I prioritize the revised list, and then I am off to the races with task one.

At first, this daily process may seem confusing or too time consuming, but it really isn't. You just need to get your mind thinking in this organized way on a regular basis. This is one reason I suggest getting up an hour earlier when you begin applying the Sacred Six process, so you can start your day off right. You will soon see how much more you get done when you begin your day with a little positivity and organization. Most people just wander through the day. The Sacred Six process gives you a plan of attack. Once you start seeing and feeling the results, the process will be easier to maintain.

Whatever method you choose to keep track of your to-dos—a notebook or a computer program—my advice is to stick with it. I see a lot of people constantly switching from system to system, which slows their progress since there is a learning curve with each new system you implement. If you believe you will see massive improvements with a different way of doing things, then change can be great, but do not change just for the sake of changing. Instead, focus on getting better at using your current system and making it second nature.

One of my mentors, Mike Lee Kanarek, is a former Israeli special forces operative who has helped me get into the best shape of my life. He gives any system 12 months to take hold; if, after that, it has not become part of his routine, he changes it. I think that's good advice. When you choose a system for your to-dos, give it about a year, and if it works, keep it going. If it doesn't, make a change.

Just be sure you are changing systems because the old way doesn't work, not just because you're bored.

Organizing Your Notes

I am looking for that address I wrote down. I know I put it somewhere. I am running around the house, looking everywhere I can think of. I yell to my wife that someone stole the address off my desk. I can't believe it's gone. I *need* that address. Ten minutes of my life are now gone because I do not have a system in place for keeping track of my notes.

I learned a long time ago from business guru Stephen Covey, author of *The 7 Habits of Highly Effective People,* that you need to keep all your notes in one place. I never thought too much about this idea until I started having the kind of senior moment I just described—at a very young age. I kept losing information I needed. It was then I remembered Covey's system. He always carried around a leather folder with a month's worth of daily calendar pages on the left side and blank pages on the right he used for his daily notes. Daily tasks and appointments were listed on the left page and on the right were phone numbers and notes on meetings, conversations, and anything else important that happened during the day. At the end of each day, he flipped the page and started the next day with a new spread.

This system allowed Covey to keep all his essential information in one place. At the end of each month he would remove the month's pages, replacing them with the new month's pages, and then put the old pages in a box labeled with the year. When the year was finished, he would have the notes from all 12 months in one place. If he ever needed to know what he was working on in January of a certain year, he just grabbed that year's box, and there were all his notes.

It was an amazing system, which I followed for about ten years. There are still times when I go back and look at those notes. The key to Covey's system is to take your time and write your daily notes legibly and in detail so that when you look back, you don't just see chicken scratches or cryptic references you can't decipher.

I have since switched from paper and a folder to an electronic notebook on my computer. Evernote software, Microsoft Word, Dropbox, and Pages for Mac are great options for this. There are more than 30 other brands of note-taking software, so you can probably find one to suit you. Paper or electronic, the idea is the same: Keep all your daily notes in one place. Note taking can be completely paperless now, and on those occasions when I still take notes with pen and paper—during a meeting, for example, because I can't type fast enough to keep up with everything I want to write down—I will later scan or take a photo of my notes to put in my electronic notebook. The added advantage of an electronic notebook is you can search by day, keyword, or topic and find information that much faster.

It is critical for your notes system to become a habit. Often people I work with tell me they have trouble quieting their minds at night so they can fall asleep. Getting a handle on your notes can help with this. Instead of tossing and turning in bed, worrying about all the things you need to do, you can keep a notebook by the bed. As soon as thoughts come, jot them down. Then you can stop thinking about them, because they will be there for you in the morning. When you get up, you can check your notebook and start taking action.

Worrying about whether or not you'll remember a thought or running around looking for where you left your notes wastes a lot of energy. The key is consistency. You need to get in the habit of keeping your notes in the same way, so that your mind can focus on other, more important things.

Calendar

The year was 1986, and I was a sophomore in high school. I watched as the instructor wrote on the blackboard, "The first tool of time management is the calendar." I dutifully wrote in my notebook, "The first tool is the calendar." At the time I was wearing a bright-orange T-shirt with matching orange shorts. I looked like a traffic cone, but hey, it was the 1980s. Just like wearing that bright-orange outfit, using the calendar as the first tool of time management is totally outdated.

The calendar does serve a purpose in the Sacred Six process, but it is not a foundational part of the process. It is simply a place to keep track of your timed appointments, such as doctor visits, yoga classes, and flight times for traveling. This is not the place to put your Sacred Six projects and tasks—items that are taking you to your dreams and require focus to get them done. They should be tracked separately from your mundane daily activities.

With the invention of the smartphone and the ease with which you can sync your calendar with your various devices, finding and using an appointment calendar you like should not be a problem. Just make sure you are using your calendar only for appointments. And when you record appointments in your calendar, make sure you also enter commute times. A calendar is most useful if it is as complete a record as possible of where you need to be throughout the day—even if where you need to be is in your car, driving to your next appointment.

When it comes to calendars, the most important rule is this: If an activity or appointment has start and end times, it goes in the calendar. If it doesn't, it belongs as a daily task.

Journal

"So let it be written. So let it be done," says Pharaoh Ramses, played by Yul Brynner, in the movie *The Ten Commandments,* referring to his minions' practice of recording the pharaoh's every word for posterity. This is one of my favorite quotes of all time. The Sacred Six process is about more than just getting things done. It is about your life story—your journey and your purpose. One of the most powerful tools you can use to document your story is a journal.

There are many ways in which a journal can help you on your journey. I think it's such an important tool that I've outlined some of the benefits.

Maintaining a Positive Mind State

A journal can help get you out of an unproductive, negative state of mind, something all of us grapple with at times, many of us on a regular basis. If you are like most people, you are your own harshest critic. You probably say things to yourself that you would never say to your best friend or even to an enemy. It is just part of who we are. The human brain evolved with a negative bias: Being more attentive to unpleasant input alerts us to danger. We all have the yin with the yang, the dark with the light.

Establishing a more positive outlook on life is a big part of the Sacred Six process. If you keep thinking, *I suck,* then you are probably going to suck. We all need to move the needle from 51 percent negative and 49 percent positive to 51 percent positive and 49 percent negative. That simple little shift can make a huge difference in achieving your dreams.

This is where the journal comes in. A simple way to start moving the needle is to record your wins on a daily basis. This means every positive thing that happens to you gets written in your journal. I like to make journal entries by hand. I keep an electronic copy also, but every year, as a gift to myself, I buy a handmade leather-bound journal that I call *The Book of Life.* I also invest in a good pen. They are both such beautiful objects that they make me want to write things down.

As my life progresses, I tell my story in my journal. I focus on not telling some negative story filled with day-to-day drama. Instead, it is a story of victories and successes. I go back once a week and read about the victories, which cements in my mind the idea that not everything that happens in life is bad.

Think about it. If you can look back at your week and see the positive things that have happened, how do you think it will help you? It is common sense, really. The more positives you can see in your life, the more positives you will be able to create in the future.

Keeping the Past in Perspective

I want to let you in on a little secret—the past and the future do not really exist. Yep, it's true. The past is gone, leaving only memory traces in the brain. The past is intangible, not real. It lives only in your mind, in your thoughts about what occurred.

The future, too, is intangible, not real. It has not happened yet. It is currently just an idea in your mind. It *will* happen, but when it does, it will be the present, not the future.

This may sound a little heady, but I'm dwelling on it to help you understand the concept of psychological time. The past is gone, and the future is yet to be. The past is typically a place of sorrow and regret. The future is often filled with worry and doubt. When you apply the Sacred Six process, you start seeing what a blessing your life really is. All you really have to work with is this moment. The only real time is now.

Without a journal, you have no structured way of remembering the past. Suppose you and I watched a play together yesterday. You may have thought it was the best play ever, and I may have thought it was terrible. If today we get into a discussion about the play, our perceptions will be different. But maybe, while we're talking, you mention something about the acting that I did not catch. In my mind, I go back and review what you're describing, and then I say, "You know, you have a point there." I am changing my past. I now think the play really wasn't so bad after all.

The point is the past is relative, and it involves our imperfect ability to recall. A journal allows us to go back and see how we were feeling and what was really going on at a particular moment in time, rather than remembering a filtered version of that moment. That is why I always recommend putting a date and time on your journal entries and including details that will jog your memory and bring you right back to that time.

Gaining Control over the Psychological Aspect of Time

Want to add years to your life? How much would that be worth to you? That's what this next power of the journal is about. If you understand the psychological aspects of time, you can slow it down.

Most of us are so caught up in the minutiae of our lives we don't actually live our lives. We think when the check comes in, or when we retire, or if we meet that perfect person, then life will be great. The truth is it's already great, and if you continue to live in the future, you are going to let life pass you by. You will be one of those people who, on their deathbeds, wonder where their lives went. People like that were never in control of their time. It was just a blur. As you get older, time just goes faster and faster—unless you learn the powerful secret of slowing time down.

You do this by becoming more aware of time. This is the power of the journal. Over the years that I have been journaling, there have been times when I got out of the habit. Maybe I let a month go by; once I let an entire year go by without journaling. What happened was that those months and years pretty much disappeared. I accomplished some things, but for the most part, I don't remember what happened.

Today I don't let months or years go by without journaling, though I do miss a few days here and there. I try to write something every single day. I write in my journal each morning, and when I do, I always flip back to the most recent entry so I can get a sense of what was going on. When I miss a few days, I find that I have not fully appreciated life during that time. I was just letting time sweep me along instead of slowing it down and enjoying it. So the key is to become aware of what is happening, slow things down enough to be present in the moment, then record what happened and reflect on it through journaling.

Being present is one of the foundational pieces of the Sacred Six process—not thinking ahead to the future or dwelling on the past but understanding this very moment is where the power is. The power is within, in your mental kingdom, not in the external, material world. Journaling to get in touch with this power will help you enjoy many more days of your life by slowing down psychological time and allowing you to fully inhabit your story.

Whether you use a paper journal or an electronic one, the intention is to get in the habit of writing an entry every day. Along with the date and time, note any significant events that can serve as memory joggers. It could be something as simple as what you were watching on TV. Personally, I tie my journal entries to sporting events. It works for me. Once you have pinpointed the day, write down the thoughts you are having.

As for recording your wins, you can do it in a few different ways. You can start each entry listing the things you are grateful for. This is a great way to kick off the day. At night before you go to bed, you can write down your wins. Or you can do both. What's most important is to start slowing down your mind so you become more present, more aware of what is happening in your life, and more focused on the positive. Then, at least once a week, go back and review your entries. If you are struggling with a lot of negativity, pull out your weekly wins and record them in a separate notebook you also review every week. That way you will have an ongoing list of wins you can refer to regularly to help you stay positive. Please do not underestimate the power of this. It can change your life.

People have used journals for thousands of years. No one else will ever be able to write about your life like you can. It does not matter how old or young you are, you can start today. Begin to capture the moments of your life, move the needle to a more positive thought process, and take control of your psychological time.

Customer Relationship Manager (CRM)

The final tool of the Sacred Six process is a CRM. In business, the term means *customer relationship management*, and it is used to store everything about customers in one place, including phone numbers, e-mail and street addresses, birth dates, social media, and more. Regardless of what you do for work, you need one of these in your life.

There are many tools you can use as your CRM. For personal contacts, I use the Apple Contacts software that came with my computer; for my business, I use the Ontraport system. There are many CRMs available, and it doesn't matter whether you choose software or an old-fashioned paper address book. What matters is that you have one place for all your contact information and that every time you get a new business card or phone number or other piece of contact information, you enter it into the system. Whatever CRM you choose, use it consistently so that just like with your notes, you know the information will be there when you need it.

TOOLS WITH A PURPOSE

You can probably tell by now the external processes that surround the Sacred Six are just as important as the internal activities of organizing your thoughts and emotions. If you are disorganized and always searching for information, phone numbers, and the like, you will not be able to find the focus or peace you need to utilize the Sacred Six process effectively.

There are so many options on the market now, you can surely find something that works for you, whether it's a new software program or paper and a pen. You can stay updated on Sacred Six-specific techniques and technology at glossinger.com. Whatever you choose, make sure you have a system in place so you are able to focus on what matters most—your mission and the steps you need to take to achieve it.

Once you have found tools that work for you, do your best to stay consistent. One of the reasons I like Apple is that the company has done such a great job of making it easy to sync information on your phone, tablet, computer, and whatever other devices you have. That makes life easier for me, so I don't have to spend a lot of time thinking about my tools. Other technologies can do something similar. The point is to find what is easiest and most efficient for you so once you get into the habit, you can keep these systems going without thinking too much about them. This is how you stay on top of your life while remaining focused and active.

You now have some tools you can use to support the process that will take you toward your dreams. There is peace in knowing you have what you need to move in the right direction. Now you are all set to recover your dreams.

CHAPTER
9

RECOVERING YOUR DREAMS

I sit patiently in my tenth-grade classroom, waiting as the teacher hands out copies of a book. I love my *Dungeons & Dragons* books and some mythology, but otherwise I am not much of a reader. That is, until I am handed this book.

As the teacher hands me the book, I look at the title: *See You at the Top. At the top of what?* I wonder. The class is a mix of study hall, gym, and sex education, so you can imagine what kinds of thoughts are going through my mind. The author's name is Zig Ziglar, which sounds like a pretty cool name to me. So I open the book.

That was the moment when everything changed for me. It was my first exposure to ideas like goals, motivations, and having a positive attitude. At the age of 15, I started to apply Ziglar's ideas and make changes in my life.

I took on a positive attitude and even switched schools. This was the birth of my ambition to be a speaker and a writer, just like Ziglar.

As I have said, I knew then what I wanted to do; what I didn't know was how a small-town kid from Indiana was going to make it happen. I didn't think I could do it. My grades were bad, and I didn't know anyone who wrote or gave speeches for a living. I also thought you had to have gray hair or be 60-plus before anyone would listen to you. There wasn't a bone in my body that believed I could ever be a speaker, much less a writer, so I spent the next 20 years living a different kind of life. And yet I dreamt.

When I finally tried to pursue my dream, I failed. Though my first book was a disaster from a marketing standpoint, I can't be too hard on it now since it eventually sold and has changed thousands of lives. Back when it came out, however, I felt as if it just confirmed what my old roommate had told me—that no one would ever listen to me.

I will never forget the day I went to speak about my book at a New Age bookstore in Fort Lauderdale, Florida. I walked in and took my place in front of 20 white chairs set up for the event. All the chairs were empty until a man who had been walking around the store sat down to listen to me. Fired up, I started. I was discussing the ideas in my book and reading excerpts from it. It seemed as though he was interested. There may have been only one person there, and 19 empty chairs, but I was loving life, until . . . the man got up and left. And there I was, speaking to 20 empty chairs. I kept going, however, because there was a voice inside telling me not to give up. I decided to give the best speech I could to those chairs. I was on my game for them, and I know those chairs were motivated, but inside I cried. My soul wept, but I kept thinking about my dream.

For many years I experienced so many doubts and fears about my dream, even some depression because of it. It was a constant battle. I was envious of other speakers who were successful. I couldn't understand why I wasn't more like them. I was giving my heart and soul, yet no one wanted to hear me. It was a horrible feeling, and I doubted whether I would ever be able to live my dream.

It really sucks to fail. It sucks when things don't work the way you want them to. Back then, I cursed God, cursed my life, and cursed my dream. I had to wonder why this dream was given to me if it was just going to become a big joke. I was lost.

Cut to ten years later, and I am sitting in the front row of a Hay House writing conference next to my wonderful writing coach, Kelly Notaras. I am watching as Reid Tracy, CEO of Hay House, and *New York Times* best-selling author Wayne Dyer discuss the writing process. I am taking copious notes, soaking up everything I can. I am in the moment and learning so much. I have finally built a business around MorningCoach.com, and thousands of people listen to me daily, but I still have not become the writer and speaker of my dreams.

As I listen to Reid and Wayne discuss writing, I can't help but think of the influence Wayne's book *Wisdom of the Ages* has had on me. As my business stumbled forward, I read a passage a day from that book, and it was one of the inspirations for MorningCoach. My daily practice of reading Wayne's book had made me think how awesome it would be if I recorded a positive audio message people could listen to every day.

As Wayne finishes his presentation, Reid takes the microphone. I am head down in my notes when I hear Reid tell the audience, "I want you to hear someone's story." Next I hear "JB Glossinger" boom out of the microphone. I look up to see Reid motioning *me* to come onstage. I love speaking, but to say I am a bit nervous is an understatement. I walk onstage and look out at the crowd and the cameras that are broadcasting this conference around the world. I take it all in.

Vince Lombardi, the great football coach and world champion, once said, "I firmly believe that any man's finest hour—his greatest fulfillment to all he holds dear—is that moment when he has worked his heart out in a good cause and lies exhausted on the field of battle, victorious." As I look out at the crowd, that is how I am feeling—victorious. I know that at least some of these people will stay, and I won't have to speak to empty chairs again. So I tell them my story.

What an amazing feeling to stand on that stage. The crowd was not there to hear me—in fact, most of them did not even know who I was. And following Wayne Dyer was a challenge in itself. I felt as if I connected with a lot of people that day. To add to my sense of victory, I joined Reid and Wayne for lunch afterward. And it all happened because I once had a dream.

In the hours I spent listening to motivational speakers on cassette tape, one person who impressed me was Nido Qubein, who came to the United States to be a motivational speaker before he had even learned to speak English. I used to listen to his tapes on sales while sitting in my old beat-up truck. Years later, I had the honor of being the keynote speaker at an event at High Point University, where Qubein was then president. After all that time I had spent dreaming of helping people just like all those wonderful speakers had helped me when I was younger, there I was, speaking after Nido Qubein. And it was all because I once had a dream.

Now, after all my failures, all my negative beliefs, here I am writing this to you. As I sit here at my desk, allowing these words to come out, there is one thing I want to make absolutely certain you take away from this book: *Don't let anyone steal your dream.* I know sometimes it may not seem as though it is going to come true. I know there will be times, probably many times, when it will be hard to believe in your dream. You may curse God, you may curse yourself, you may even curse life itself, but don't let your dream die.

There is a popular saying: "Do what you love, and the money will follow." I really believe that's true, but it doesn't always follow right away. What happens when you are doing what you love, and it is not working for you? That is frustrating. It can feel as if you are chasing a rainbow to find the pot of gold, only to have the pot of gold move as soon as you get there. And then move again. And again.

One of the hardest things about building an amazing life is patience. If you have children, you don't really notice their growth on a daily basis because you are too close. However, if you don't see a friend's child for a few years or even a few months, you notice right away how much he or she has grown. Our personal development is a lot like that. We don't always notice the gains we are making. But if you make a sincere effort to improve, you are almost sure to succeed.

So dream. The size of the dream doesn't matter; just allow yourself to dream. Don't let others get in your way. Don't get in your own way. Keep moving forward, step-by-step, day by day. That is the most important action you can take toward meeting your goals and recovering your dreams.

Make Space for Your Dreams

For years I lived with my yellow Labrador, Niko, and my German shepherd mix, Kaos. They were two wonderful companions who filled my life with joy and energy. They also filled my house with dog hair, so much so that I had to vacuum every day to keep up with it all. Until I bought a special vacuum designed to deal with pet hair, I used a regular vacuum that would clog up quickly and lose suction.

Dreaming can be like that. If you have lost sight of your dream, then you need to understand the Vacuum Law of Prosperity. Think about Niko and Kaos and all that hair that fills the vacuum canister until it can't hold any more. That same thing can happen to us. Most of us have lives so filled with minutiae that there isn't room for anything else. That is why it is so important to release whatever is in your way. You have to make space for dreams.

Hoarders, a popular television show, features people who literally hang on to all their garbage. They fill their houses with it because they are emotionally attached to all those things. And because of their emotional attachment they live in what looks like a garbage dump. This is an extreme example of what I'm talking about, but think about it: With all that garbage, how can anything new come into their lives?

One of the first things I had to do to live my dream was to create a vacuum. I left my job. I did it on faith, and I failed—at first. The vacuum I created was eventually filled, and I'm glad I took the steps that I did. Knowing what I know now, I probably could have gotten there a different, less painful way. I could have kept my job and worked on my dream at night. Still, I created a vacuum, which was a necessary part of the process.

Now is a good time to think about where your life is clogged up. What is keeping you from recovering your dreams?

Practice Letting Go

Over the next couple of days, why not do a few things to create a vacuum in your life that can be filled with dreaming? Start by literally cleaning out your closets. If you have not worn an article of clothing in more than a year, donate it. If it is your wedding dress or tuxedo, then you can keep it, but everything else you're not wearing should go.

Next clean out your car and your garage. Then move on to the rest of the house. Let go of anything that is physically cluttering up your life and getting in your way. I know you may be attached to some of these things, but they are clogging your dream vacuum. You need to learn to let go. If, while cleaning out, you encounter some emotional baggage you also need to let go, then seek out a therapist or medical professional to help you work through your issues. This is important because the bottom line is it is time to create room for something new in your life.

While you are cleaning things out, visualize all the dog hair in the vacuum canister and think about what is holding you back from your dreams. Focus on the *why* we talked about in Chapter 5.

Why does this process work? Because nature abhors a vacuum. Where there is a void, something naturally will move in to fill it. If you take all the clothes out of your closet and give them away, that closet will fill up again eventually. It's the same with the Vacuum Law of Prosperity. When you clear space for new things, new things will inevitably come into your life.

A side benefit of letting go of what no longer serves you is when you're done going through your closets and garage, everything will be clean and organized, which will make you feel so much better. Who doesn't feel awesome when everything is in its place, ready to go? Throughout the Sacred Six process, you always want to be working to stay organized and on top of things. If you have a stack of dirty dishes in the sink, what typically happens when you dirty another dish? You just stack it on top of the others. If you have been cleaning the dishes as you use them, then when you dirty another dish, you're more likely to wash it and put it away.

From this moment on, dedicate yourself to keeping space open in your life. Keep your desk clean and your environment organized. Make sure your vacuum doesn't get clogged. This is what is going to allow those dreams to start manifesting in your life.

Envy

Walking into the Jaguar dealership, my mind was focused on the task at hand. I had read if you put things on a dream board and looked at them every day, then the Law of Attraction would take effect. I was in the process of building my personal dream board, and I needed a picture of the Jaguar that I wanted. Beyond that, the book I was reading said I also had to take the car I wanted out for a test drive. I had a nasty feeling in the pit of my stomach as I walked into the showroom to ask about the car. I was a bundle of nerves because I knew I couldn't afford the car, and so did the salesman. He had seen me drive up in my old pickup truck.

As I approached, the salesman looked at me and said, "May I help you?" I could feel his disgust as he said it. I shivered and replied, "Yes, I would like to drive that Jaguar over there." He laughed and said, "If you want to drive it, first you have to learn how to say it. It is called a Jag–yoo–ar." I looked at him, perplexed, and tried to mimic what he had said. He turned around and told me, "When you can pronounce it, you can drive it."

My shoulders must have dropped three inches at that moment. I felt so defeated by that salesman. He had obviously been a real jerk, but that wasn't what pissed me off the most. It was my lack of presence and strength. I knew I could not afford the car, and I knew going in I would not get the picture or the ride that I wanted. As I was standing there, another guy around my age came in. The salesman walked right up to him, and they started talking. I watched as the two of them went out to the parking lot, got into a brand-new Jag–yoo–ar, and went for a ride. I was so angry and so filled with envy. Why was God doing this to me? Why do some people have money and others don't? Why do some people get to live their dreams? After that day, I would get angry whenever I saw nice cars, nice houses, even well-dressed people. I had so much frustration and anger over feeling like a failure that I took it out on other people. For a long time, I didn't understand the lesson that life was giving me that day.

In order to live my dreams, I needed to become someone different, not just financially but also deep within myself. I couldn't just wear a fake Rolex and expect girls would be impressed enough to date me as a result. Obviously, I never got one date because of my watch. As they say in golf, "It's not the clubs; it's the operator." What I really needed was a good long look in the mirror.

In order to manifest your dreams, you have to *become* your dreams. I am happily married now, but if I put on that fake Rolex today, I don't think anyone would even look at it or, if they did, would question whether it was real because of who I have become. The operator—me—has grown up and become so much more than I thought I could ever be at that time. And that Jag–yoo–ar? Well, as I told you in Chapter 3, I got one, and I still pronounce it the same way I did back then: *Jag–wahr.* And as we now know, it wasn't the Jaguar that was my true dream.

When it comes to dreams, it can be difficult to break free from our past conditioning. Much of the Sacred Six process focuses on that. It is a game plan to help you grow as a person, and it gives you the steps you need to make improvements on a daily basis. Those improvements won't always show up in the material universe. A lot of the work is done internally, which is why you have to keep that journal rocking and remember to celebrate your victories along the way. That's what will keep you going. You may feel frustrated or envious at times, but that's okay. You just have to learn to release those feelings when they come. It doesn't hurt to have a little Jag–yoo–ar motivation once in a while. Just don't let it slow you down, overwhelm you with negativity, or fill your mind with doubts.

Doubts were among the biggest challenges I had. I used to think other people had received some special blessing or were luckier than me. I couldn't figure out why I was living in my shitty little hovel—my one-bedroom apartment in Tucson—while other people seemed to be thriving. I was always battling doubt. I kept seeing the world as filled with people who were succeeding—practically everyone except me. I couldn't figure out how I would ever live my dreams.

Tactics for Battling Self-Doubt

If you are stuck feeling envious and frustrated, I guarantee that these two methods can change your life.

1) Borrowing the Belief of Others

Read biographies and watch documentaries, especially about performers. As a speaker onstage, I consider myself an artist, and there are two kinds of people I love to watch and learn from: comedians and rock stars. I believe comedy is the most difficult form of speech there is. It takes energy and intellect and an ability to read the crowd. Rock stars have to have the *it* factor. They have to bring energy and charisma to hold the audience's attention and rev them up.

When I was living in my hovel and dreaming of being a speaker who could hold an audience, I thought about how comedians and rock stars did just that. I didn't believe for a minute I could actually live my dream, but I still wanted to. So I watched documentaries or read stories about people who had succeeded in these areas, and I was amazed to discover how many of them had once lived in hovels of their own. Most of them succeeded through hard work, persistence, and determination. I had all those qualities; I just didn't have the belief in myself. However, as I read their stories, I was able to start believing more. I was borrowing the belief of others.

I still get inspiration from biographies and documentaries. One of the documentaries I watched recently was *God Bless Ozzy Osbourne*, about the rocker Ozzy Osbourne and his wife, Sharon. If you look at the rise of Ozzy Osbourne and his attempts at self-destruction as he battled his demons, you can see a man who had real self-esteem issues. I felt the pain that the craziest man in 1980s and 1990s rock and roll experienced, and I identified with his suffering. In a sense, the alcohol and drugs he used were an escape from his life. At many points in my own life, I did the same thing, though perhaps not to the same extreme.

I watched with sorrow as Sharon discussed what was going on behind the scenes: the challenges, the fights, the family falling apart—things we did not see in the news or even on their famous reality TV show, *The Osbournes*. As their son, Jack, said in the documentary, "No one wants to watch a show about a family being torn apart by alcoholism." What everyone was seeing wasn't the truth; it was what the producers wanted us to see.

We all have issues and demons, even if the world can't always see them. When you are struggling with your own problems, other people may seem bulletproof. That is why watching documentaries or reading biographies is critical. It is a kind of reality check. It shows you everyone struggles and no one is bulletproof, but people still succeed despite it all.

I learned a lot from Sharon Osbourne, too. What a genius that woman is. She held the whole enterprise together with strength and courage. She was able to be a parent while building the Osbourne brand and helping her husband through his hard times. I know you may be thinking, *But, JB, they had millions of dollars, and Ozzy is so famous.* They didn't start out that way. A reaction like that is your ego getting in the way of seeing and learning from what other human beings have gone through. Don't let those thoughts creep in; they are the kind that defeated me year after year.

The best thing to do when your self-confidence starts to wane is to find people you can borrow belief from. Find people in your field you can look up to—and learn what it really took for those people to get to where they are today. Everyone else who has reached a level of success and achieved their dream has had to fight battles and demons.

To help you with your own struggles, make a commitment to read a biography a month for a year. That will give you 12 stories, 12 people whose belief you can borrow. Commit to watching documentaries, as well. I try to watch one a week. It helps me discover new things and borrow belief when I need it. This practice has become one of the most important learning experiences in my life.

2) Masterminding

The other tactic that has helped me tremendously in overcoming self-doubt is Masterminding. The term *mastermind* comes from the author and thought leader Napoleon Hill, who described it as "a mind that is developed through the harmonious cooperation of two or more people who ally themselves for the purpose of accomplishing any given task." A Mastermind group is a form of peer mentoring popular with successful businesspeople.

When I started my MorningCoach business, I didn't think I needed any outside help, which was just sheer arrogance. I was the Morning*Coach*, after all. That was my ego getting in the way, along with the fact that I was broke at the time and didn't think I could afford to invest in any kind of support. Today, I give a lot of credit to the Mastermind groups I'm in. The ideas and coaching I've received from people in these groups have led to some of the biggest breakthroughs in my life.

Masterminding is a mental challenge. You get to see the people in your group doing all these amazing things. You get to know these people, and, if you have the right facilitator, some of them will become like family. Then you see them put on their shoes and socks each morning the same way you do. They aren't much different from you. That alone can give you the belief you need to succeed. And then the ideas and coaching these people bring to the table can really help you overcome your own hurdles.

You can start a Mastermind group yourself, or you can find one that already exists. The key to a great Mastermind is to have a good facilitator, so if you are looking for a Mastermind group, make sure to interview the person who is putting it together.

I also think it's a good idea to make sure there is an entry fee to belong. In my experience, free Masterminds don't work. If people are not paying to be there, they start finding other things to do instead. Great Masterminds can run anywhere from a few thousand dollars a year to six figures. What you choose depends on where you are financially. If you are making millions of dollars a year, you probably wouldn't want to be in a Mastermind with people making a few thousand dollars. There wouldn't be much for you to relate to. That is why many Masterminds have an income qualifier, so that everyone gets the most out of the experience. Clearly fees like that are out of reach for many people, as they were for me for years. If that's true for you, you could form your own Mastermind with others who have limited funds. If you do this, I still suggest you require members to put a least a nominal fee in the pot—$10 or $20—even if you have to stretch a little.

As you grow personally and financially, you can pick and choose which Mastermind you want to participate in. I am in three Masterminds currently, and run one myself called the Inner Circle. Together they have helped me change my business and my life. Mastermind is one of the best investments I have ever made. If you are just starting out, I suggest finding one that already exists instead of attempting to start your own.

WHEN DO YOU QUIT ON A DREAM?

My bank account is going to be in the red again, and the checks I've just written are going to bounce. This is all I can think about. I am anxious and desperate. I don't know why I left my job. I didn't think it through. I just acted on impulse, as I have so many times in my life. I took a big risk this time and put myself and my wife in danger as a result. I close my eyes and think about all the mistakes I've made. *Can I survive this?* I wonder. *My dream of being a writer and speaker is failing. Where is the money going to come from? Is it time to throw in the towel?*

Shifting from a paycheck mentality to an entrepreneurial mentality was one of the biggest alterations I had to make. In order to live my dream, I had to fight through the constraints of the world we live in. I couldn't get health insurance. I didn't know when more money would be coming in. I had to figure out how to survive. Suddenly, I found myself wishing for that paycheck again, even though I had hated the job it came with.

Sitting in my chair, looking at the red in my checking account and the stack of bills on my desk, I thought about picking up the phone and calling a recruiter. That was my moment of truth. Instead I got up and went for a walk to clear my head. When I returned, I looked at the thousands of books written by my mentors and guides. If they could do it, so could I. I believed I could make it, and somehow I would find the money. I was not giving up on my dream.

You shouldn't have to put yourself in such dire circumstances. If I had set myself up and formulated a plan, I wouldn't have been in that situation. That is why tools, teachers, mentors, and Masterminds are so important. They can help you find a workable path to your dreams so you don't have to fight through the need to quit.

But when does the dream become too much? When have you become so myopically focused on your dream it's hurting you? I can answer only from my own experience.

Any rational person who looked at my situation back then would have told me to give up and get a job. But if I had done that, I wouldn't be writing these words today. There could be a time to throw in the towel, but based on my own experience, I don't know when that would be. My belief is there is no dream that is too myopic, unless it runs counter to common sense. If, for example, my dream were to play NBA basketball for the Miami Heat, well, at 5'9", 150 pounds, and 46 years of age, that would be virtually impossible. Okay, Tyrone "Muggsy" Bogues was only 5'3" yet he had a 15-year career in the NBA. However, he was a phenom, and I was never the ball player he was. If, however, I wanted to work for the Heat organization, that would be a dream worth pursuing.

My point here is unless your dream is utterly beyond reason, then you must not give up. Miracles happen. I know you are smart enough to separate the truly impossible from what you may be framing as impossible when, with hard work, it is not. If you had been my high school grammar teacher, you would have thought that my writing a book would be impossible, but you are holding proof it was not.

I have a friend in Miami named Eddie Rodriquez who dresses up in a bunny suit and works to make people laugh and be happy. He actually created a company called Smile and Wave America. Eddie has walked from Miami to Washington, D.C., smiling and waving at people along the way. There is not a lot of money in smiling and waving. In fact, Eddie also owns a construction company, which is how he makes money to live on. His dream is to help people be happy and to build a business based on that idea. And that's the dream he works toward.

Many people are too cool to appreciate Eddie. They just don't get what he does. Eddie keeps going after his dream. He keeps bringing smiles and waves into the Universe. Should Eddie quit because he hasn't yet reached his goal of financial gain? Should Eddie give up because some members of society don't get him, or even take advantage of him sometimes? I don't think so. I, for one, love to see Eddie making the world a better place. I would be the last person to say he is myopic or fooling himself. In fact, I believe the world needs more people like Eddie Rodriquez.

Envision a single mother on welfare who dreams of being a writer. She struggles with rejection slips but keeps going forward. She finally sells her book for the equivalent of $4,000. Her name is J. K. Rowling, and her first book was *Harry Potter and the Sorcerer's Stone.* Imagine if she had quit! I recently visited Universal Orlando in Florida, and half the park is now Harry Potter themed. Rowling's vision has become a reality. And not just her own reality but reality for millions, if not billions, of people around the world.

What is the difference between Ozzy Osbourne, J. K. Rowling, Eddie Rodriquez, and you? Not much. They just stuck with their dreams. That is what the Sacred Six process is about. It is about building a life and living that life. The struggles and the challenges are all part of it either way. And as I keep saying, your life is your story—yours and no one else's. So why not write it yourself?

"Thoughts are things, beliefs make them so, and actions solidify beliefs": This is something I say all the time. It means that we must nourish our dreams like plants in a garden. If we allow the negative to take over, it will be as if weeds are choking the plants. The key to maintaining a dream is to strengthen your belief. From there, what's critical is the daily work you put in.

I held on to my dream over the years and kept taking action, but the belief that I could do it wasn't there. Then, as the belief started to come, my dream began to materialize. The magic happened when more people started to believe. When I first launched MorningCoach and only a few people were listening, it was really hard to keep moving forward. I was filled with self-doubt. But then, as my audience grew and things began to happen for my listeners, my belief grew. I'm convinced the support of my listeners led to the manifestation of my dream. Rowling probably believed her book could be good, but if she is like most writers, she had some doubts. Do you think she has doubts now? Do you think *I* doubt I can write a book now? I'm getting closer to more of my dreams as I type these words on the page.

I have shared the trials and tribulations I have gone through to live my dreams so that you can find an easier path to yours. I have laid out a process to take you there. Now all you have to do is start working it. If you don't yet 100 percent believe in yourself or your dream, that's okay. Just follow the steps. Recognize that others have been where you are and they have succeeded, just as you can.

Focus on moving forward. Focus on your dreams. Get your Sacred Six in place. The world needs your energy, talent, and love. This is what is going to make a difference for you and the world around you.

CONCLUSION

Throughout these pages, the focus has been on recovering your dreams and living the life you have imagined. Much of what I have laid out is a straightforward guide to the journey, with step-by-step exercises and practical advice for reaching your cherished goals. I don't want you to think that the Sacred Six process is only about the journey and not the destination. Ultimately, the process is about transformation and the promise of an awakened life—one in which mission, values, and goals are in full alignment.

At its core, the Sacred Six process supports us in viewing life with the eyes of the Observer, the true self, which is open, eternal, and unchanging, and leaving the demanding, egoist, conditioned mind behind. Accessing the Observer is not only the basis for making wise decisions but a critical factor in discovering what you really want and what you truly value.

One of my personal day-to-day goals is finding peace. Often I am so focused on helping others realize their dreams that I get stuck in the minutiae of life and lose any semblance of a peaceful mind. Like many people, I find it's the small things that trip me up: haggling over the design of my website, trying to get it right; jockeying for a tee time at the golf course on a busy day; managing a little road rage that threatens to spoil my commute. Whatever pressures I encounter in the day-to-day, the Sacred Six has tools I rely on to restore my naturally positive outlook and sense of joy.

When I feel myself being pulled off center, I turn to one of the Finding Peace techniques described in Chapter 6. Cleansing Breath is particularly effective for bringing peace of mind in the midst of daily chaos. Perhaps nothing is more critical than being at peace, because when we are not, we are unable to access the truth and happiness that life has to offer. It doesn't matter what it is that throws us off course. One of my favorite teachings from *A Course in Miracles* says, "There are no small upsets. They are all equally disturbing to my peace of mind."

This daily struggle to find peace is one of the reasons I put the Sacred Six together in the first place. I know with a plan, a clear mind, and an understanding of psychological time, living a peaceful life is possible. What we focus on expands, and what better to focus on than peace? Once we focus on it, it will come.

You now have a process for manifesting the life experience you desire. So go forth and receive all the love, joy, and happiness you have longed for. You deserve it!

JB Glossinger
Fort Lauderdale, Florida
May 2016

APPENDIX

I

VALUES LIST

This list of 417 values was put together
by my friend Steve Pavlina. It is a helpful
resource for creating your own values list, an
exercise in Chapter 4 (see page 63).

Abundance
Acceptance
Accessibility
Accomplishment
Accountability
Accuracy
Achievement
Acknowledgment
Activeness
Adaptability
Adoration
Adroitness
Advancement
Adventure
Affection
Affluence
Aggressiveness
Agility
Alertness
Altruism
Amazement
Ambition
Amusement
Anticipation
Appreciation
Approachability
Approval
Art
Articulacy
Artistry
Assertiveness
Assurance
Attentiveness
Attractiveness
Audacity
Availability

Awareness
Awe
Balance
Beauty
Being the best
Belonging
Benevolence
Bliss
Boldness
Bravery
Brilliance
Buoyancy
Calmness
Camaraderie
Candor
Capability
Care
Carefulness
Celebrity
Certainty
Challenge
Change
Charity
Charm
Chastity
Cheerfulness
Clarity
Cleanliness
Clear-mindedness
Cleverness
Closeness
Comfort
Commitment
Community
Compassion
Competence

Competition
Completion
Composure
Concentration
Confidence
Conformity
Congruency
Connection
Consciousness
Conservation
Consistency
Contentment
Continuity
Contribution
Control
Conviction
Conviviality
Coolness
Cooperation
Cordiality
Correctness
Country
Courage
Courtesy
Craftiness
Creativity
Credibility
Cunning
Curiosity
Daring
Decisiveness
Decorum
Deference
Delight
Dependability
Depth

Desire	Euphoria	Frugality
Determination	Excellence	Fun
Devotion	Excitement	Gallantry
Devoutness	Exhilaration	Generosity
Dexterity	Expectancy	Gentility
Dignity	Expediency	Giving
Diligence	Experience	Grace
Direction	Expertise	Gratitude
Directness	Exploration	Gregariousness
Discipline	Expressiveness	Growth
Discovery	Extravagance	Guidance
Discretion	Extroversion	Happiness
Diversity	Exuberance	Harmony
Dominance	Fairness	Health
Dreaming	Faith	Heart
Drive	Fame	Helpfulness
Duty	Family	Heroism
Dynamism	Fascination	Holiness
Eagerness	Fashion	Honesty
Ease	Fearlessness	Honor
Economy	Ferocity	Hopefulness
Ecstasy	Fidelity	Hospitality
Education	Fierceness	Humility
Effectiveness	Financial	Humor
Efficiency	independence	Hygiene
Elation	Firmness	Imagination
Elegance	Fitness	Impact
Empathy	Flexibility	Impartiality
Encouragement	Flow	Independence
Endurance	Fluency	Individuality
Energy	Focus	Industry
Enjoyment	Fortitude	Influence
Entertainment	Frankness	Ingenuity
Enthusiasm	Freedom	Inquisitiveness
Environmentalism	Friendliness	Insightfulness
Ethics	Friendship	Inspiration

Integrity	Meticulousness	Potency
Intellect	Mindfulness	Power
Intelligence	Modesty	Practicality
Intensity	Motivation	Pragmatism
Intimacy	Mysteriousness	Precision
Intrepidness	Nature	Preparedness
Introspection	Neatness	Presence
Introversion	Nerve	Pride
Intuition	Nonconformity	Privacy
Intuitiveness	Obedience	Proactivity
Inventiveness	Open-mindedness	Professionalism
Investing	Openness	Prosperity
Involvement	Optimism	Prudence
Joy	Order	Punctuality
Judiciousness	Organization	Purity
Justice	Originality	Rationality
Keenness	Outdoors	Realism
Kindness	Outlandishness	Reason
Knowledge	Outrageousness	Reasonableness
Leadership	Partnership	Recognition
Learning	Patience	Recreation
Liberation	Passion	Refinement
Liberty	Peace	Reflection
Lightness	Perceptiveness	Relaxation
Liveliness	Perfection	Reliability
Logic	Perkiness	Relief
Longevity	Perseverance	Religiousness
Love	Persistence	Reputation
Loyalty	Persuasiveness	Resilience
Majesty	Philanthropy	Resolution
Making a difference	Piety	Resolve
Marriage	Playfulness	Resourcefulness
Mastery	Pleasantness	Respect
Maturity	Pleasure	Responsibility
Meaning	Poise	Rest
Meekness	Polish	Restraint
Mellowness	Popularity	Reverence

Richness
Rigor
Sacredness
Sacrifice
Sagacity
Saintliness
Sanguinity
Satisfaction
Science
Security
Self-control
Selflessness
Self-reliance
Self-respect
Sensitivity
Sensuality
Serenity
Service
Sexiness
Sexuality
Sharing
Shrewdness
Significance
Silence
Silliness
Simplicity
Sincerity
Skillfulness
Solidarity
Solitude
Sophistication
Soundness
Speed
Spirit
Spirituality
Spontaneity

Spunk
Stability
Status
Stealth
Stillness
Strength
Structure
Success
Support
Supremacy
Surprise
Sympathy
Synergy
Teaching
Teamwork
Temperance
Thankfulness
Thoroughness
Thoughtfulness
Thrift
Tidiness
Timeliness
Traditionalism
Tranquility
Transcendence
Trust
Trustworthiness
Truth
Understanding
Unflappability
Uniqueness
Unity
Usefulness
Utility
Valor
Variety

Victory
Vigor
Virtue
Vision
Vitality
Vivacity
Volunteering
Warmheartedness
Warmth
Watchfulness
Wealth
Willfulness
Willingness
Winning
Wisdom
Wittiness
Wonder
Worthiness
Youthfulness

APPENDIX

II

DESIGNING A SACRED SIX DAILY PLAN

In Chapter 7, we looked at how to break goals and projects into daily tasks. Here are two more examples of how to set up a Sacred Six daily plan.

MATTHEW: STAY-AT-HOME DAD

Matthew is a 34-year-old stay-at-home father looking to make life better for his family. He has a good marriage, but the loving feeling is starting to dissipate as his wife increasingly complains she is pulling all the weight. Over the years Matthew has let himself go physically, so now he has decided to get back in shape and focus on losing some of the extra weight.

As a rule, exercise should not be one of your Sacred Six projects; my reasoning is that for most people, exercise is just a normal part of everyday life. However, it can become a Sacred Six project if, as in Matthew's case, one of your top priority goals is to get in shape and adding daily exercise would be part of a noticeable life change. In Matthew's case exercise will remain a Sacred Six goal until exercising becomes a habit, something as routine as grocery shopping. At that point he will replace exercising with another goal.

Given his mission of improving life with his family and getting back in shape physically, here are the goals Matthew came up with:

1. Lose ten pounds over the next nine months.
2. Add $1,000 a month income.
3. Learn how to cook to better his family's health and his own.
4. Become more organized about finances and understand finances.

After determining his goals are aligned with his current mission and his values—family, friends, sports, freedom, and doing the right thing—Matthew breaks his goals into projects:

Goal 1: Lose ten pounds over the next nine months.

☐ Project: Hire a trainer and join a gym.

☐ Project: Make exercise part of lifestyle.

☐ Project: Find an accountability partner.

Goal 2: Add $1,000 a month income.

☐ Project: Look at residual revenue opportunities. (Residual revenue is passive income from sources like royalties on book sales, software licenses, usage fees for music, actors' payments for commercials that air. I think of this as making money while you sleep, rather than trading hours for dollars.)

☐ Project: Hire a career coach.

☐ Project: Buy/borrow books on working from home and read them.

Goal 3: Learn how to cook to improve his family's health and his own.

☐ Project: Take a cooking class.

☐ Project: Buy/borrow and read some recipe books.

Goal 4. Become more organized about finances and more financially savvy.

☐ Project: Take a class on organizing finances.

☐ Project: Find three podcasts to listen to on personal finance.

Matthew has identified ten projects that could take him toward his goals. Because the Sacred Six process limits him to pursuing just six projects at a time, he will have to prioritize. One way he can do so is to review each of the projects on his list and ask himself, *Is this an ongoing project, or something I will do just once and be done?*

After prioritizing, Matthew settles on the following Sacred Six projects:

1. Hire a trainer and join a gym.
2. Hire a career coach.
3. Find an accountability partner.
4. Make exercise a part of the lifestyle.
5. Take a class on organizing finances.
6. Take a cooking class.

Matthew has several one-shot projects he can clear immediately: hiring a trainer, hiring a career coach, joining a gym, and finding an accountability partner. I recommend doing quick projects like this first, so you can focus on projects that will take more time.

As Matthew completes each onetime project and checks it off Sacred Six list, he can replace it with another project from his longer list of ten. Whenever you add a new Sacred Six project, it's a good idea to reprioritize the list, based on what is currently most important to you.

Breaking down Matthew's Sacred Six projects, here's how he set up his Sacred Six daily plan:

1. Hire a trainer and join a gym.

This is Matthew's first priority project for working on his goal of losing ten pounds over the next nine months. I would suggest he find a gym close to home. Research shows that proximity and convenience are the two main factors in determining whether or not people keep going to the gym. Matthew should interview a few trainers, then pick one and get to work. A few sessions with a trainer may even come with his new gym membership. This project doesn't require daily tasks, but he needs to get it out of the way as soon as possible.

2. Hire a career coach.

For this project, Matthew's daily task is finding a coach. He can search the Internet or ask for recommendations from friends. This is another project that will fall off his list quickly and be replaced.

3. Find an accountability partner.

Matthew needs a buddy to support him in keeping his commitment to exercise. His daily task is to go on social media or reach out to friends or the MorningCoach community to find someone to hold his feet to the fire.

4. Make exercise a part of the lifestyle.

Here's where the daily tasks really kick in. Because Matthew's mission is to get into better shape and his goal is to lose ten pounds, one of his priority projects is to make exercise a regular part of his life. His daily task, therefore, is to exercise every day until it becomes habitual. How long it will take for exercise to become a habit depends on the individual. In general it takes between a few months and a year. Once Matthew turns exercise into a habit, this project will come off his daily task list and be replaced.

5. Take a class on organizing finances.

To fulfill his goal of become more organized about his finances, Matthew has set a project of taking a class. His first daily task would be to find a class and enroll. As an ongoing daily task, he can put his class lessons into action. He also needs to make tracking and organizing his finances a daily habit, and he should be working on developing an investment mind-set—using money to make money, instead of spending it on things. Every dollar he spends should deliver a return. I would also advise him to build a budget worksheet and review it every morning.

6. Take a cooking class.

This is one of Matthew's priority projects toward his goal of learning to cook to improve his family's health and his own. His daily tasks would be to find and enroll in a cooking class, and then to cook something every day. Eventually he will become a better and more confident cook, and at that point, he can check this project off his list. He will continue to cook for his family every day, and if cooking becomes a passion, he may decide to take more courses and continue to learn so he can expand his repertoire in the kitchen. If so, this project and its related tasks would stay on his Sacred Six project list indefinitely.

RICKY: PURSUING A PASSION

Ricky is a 38-year-old salesman who has always dreamed of playing the piano, but with his sales job, he doesn't know when he will find time. After listening to the MorningCoach.com podcast, he decides to give it a shot. He is also focused on making more money at work and finding more time into his life. His mission is to build his life around his passions and his values—spirituality, family, music, and travel—and to increase his income.

He has set the following goals:

1. Learn to play the piano.
2. Get up an hour earlier to organize in order to have more time.
3. Build up sales territory for additional revenue, aiming at double-digit growth in six months.

Here are the projects Ricky came up with to move him toward those goals:

Goal 1: Learn to play the piano.

- ☐ Project: Find a piano instructor.
- ☐ Project: Google *keyboards* and read reviews.
- ☐ Project: Buy or rent an electronic keyboard.
- ☐ Project: Buy/borrow books and magazines on playing piano.

Goal 2: Get up an hour earlier to organize in order to have more time.

- ☐ Project: Set alarm clock one hour earlier.
- ☐ Project: Listen to MorningCoach every day.

Goal 3: Build sales territory for additional revenue, aiming at double-digit growth in six months.

- ☐ Project: Focus on improving sales figures at work and building sales relationships.
- ☐ Project: Study the 80/20 rule and focus on growing revenue on a per customer basis.

Ricky has a good base of projects to start from to manifest his dream of playing the piano. If he can accomplish his goal of getting up early, the result will be a keystone habit that will have a positive effect on other areas of his life. Improving his performance at work and increasing sales will remove some financial stress, freeing him to focus on his real passion, learning the piano.

After he prioritizes his projects, Ricky's Sacred Six list looks like this:

1.   Set alarm one hour earlier.
2.   Find a piano instructor.
3.   Google *keyboards* and read reviews.
4.   Focus on improving sales figures at work and building sales relationships.
5.   Buy/borrow books and magazines on playing the piano.
6.   Listen to MorningCoach every day.

You might wonder why Ricky hasn't included "Buy or rent keyboard" in his Sacred Six daily tasks. He has to research keyboards before he can buy or rent one. Once he has read the reviews, he can check off that project and replace it with "Buy or rent keyboard."

Breaking down his Sacred Six projects, here's how Ricky might lay out the tasks in his Sacred Six daily plan:

1. Set alarm one hour earlier.

In this case, Ricky's project and daily task are the same. Setting his alarm so he gets up an hour earlier will prepare him for a more productive day. Once the daily task becomes a habit, Ricky can take it off his list and move on to a new project.

2. Find a piano instructor.

This is a priority to reach Ricky's goal of learning to play piano. The daily task is to use all avenues to find the right person, including searching online and soliciting recommendations from friends. In situations like this, I have found it helpful to join an online forum for input from people who share your interest. Once Ricky draws up a short list of instructors, he could take a private lesson from each to get a feel for their methods. After he picks an instructor, his task will be to take weekly lessons. Since finding an instructor should take only a few weeks to accomplish, this project will then be replaced by lessons and daily practice.

3. Google and read reviews on keyboards.

This is a fun project. Ricky gets to pick out a keyboard. He can get suggestions from people on relevant online forums, then go to a few stores, get advice from the sales staff, and test some keyboards. Or he may decide to wait for advice from his instructor. This project will take just a few weeks and then be replaced with daily practice.

4. Focus on sales numbers at work and building sales relationships.

This is not a project that will take Ricky toward his mission of learning to play the piano, but it is an important work project that is part of his mission. He will focus on developing the relationship aspect of his job. This could be done six to eight hours a day since it is what is currently earning him money. He can gather information he needs to turn prospects into sales. This project is critical to Ricky's personal growth and performance at work. I would break it into smaller chunks, creating five or six tasks he can work on over the course of his day.

5. Buy/borrow some books and magazines on piano.

I believe in immersing yourself in whatever you want to learn. When I wanted to improve my golf game, I surrounded myself with all things golf. I watched the Golf Channel on TV, read every golf magazine and book I could find, and transformed my house into a golf center. Ricky could do something similar with the piano. Buying and borrowing books and subscribing to magazines should take only a few days. Then he can replace that daily task with one like spending 30 minutes a day reading the books and magazines.

6. Listen to MorningCoach every day.

This is an easy task as Ricky will just plug into MorningCoach.com every morning and focus on the teachings. He can put this first on his daily schedule and check it off his list each morning.

ACKNOWLEDGMENTS

First, my thanks to all the members of the Morning-Coach community. Without you this would not be possible.

Writing a book is one thing; building a book is another. So thanks to all the wonderful people who helped along the way.

To Reid Tracy at Hay House, who had the vision to take this book on, and Lindsay DiGianvittorio and Joan Duncan Oliver, my editors, who were a writer's dream to work with.

To Kelly Notaras, one of the best writing coaches in the world.

To Christa Bourg, who helped shape the book and bring it life.

To my team, Jeremy Bernabe, Leah McAllister, and Margarita Rodriquez. What a strange journey this has been. I thank you for being a part of it.

To Luis Rosario for all his help.

To those magical teachers who taught me so much: Zig Ziglar, Wayne Dyer, Randy Gage, Tony Robbins, Les Brown, and Michael Singer.

To my Inner Circle, you guys just rock. I love each and every one of you. You are truly the band I have always dreamed of.

To all the readers of this book, I thank you and acknowledge you for helping make the world a better place.

And to my grammar teacher, who gave me a D in grammar along with years of anguish and fear, and who said I couldn't write: thank you for the motivation.

ABOUT THE AUTHOR

JB Glossinger, M.B.A., Ph.D., is an internationally known visionary, motivational speaker, author, coach, and consultant who helps individuals, businesses, and organizations manifest their visions. A modern-day life archeologist who brings esoteric wisdom to the general public, he is one of only a handful of people to hold both an M.B.A. degree and a Ph.D. in metaphysics.

JB is the host of a daily podcast, MorningCoach.com, that reaches 15,000 listeners in more than 100 countries around the globe. Reaching number one in the health category on iTunes after just three weeks of broadcasting, it continues to be one of the top 20 podcasts in the world.

JB is a contributing writer for *The Business Journals,* a network of 43 newspapers and online publications. He has more than 200,000 followers on his social media accounts. For further information on JB, you can visit glossinger.com.

Hay House Titles of Related Interest

YOU CAN HEAL YOUR LIFE, the movie, starring Louise Hay &
Friends
(available as a 1-DVD program and an expanded 2-DVD set)
Watch the trailer at: www.LouiseHayMovie.com

THE SHIFT, the movie,
starring Dr. Wayne W. Dyer
(available as a 1-DVD program and an expanded 2-DVD set)
Watch the trailer at: www.DyerMovie.com

All of the above are available at your local bookstore,
or may be ordered by contacting Hay House (see next page).

***

We hope you enjoyed this Hay House book. If you'd like to receive our online catalog featuring additional information on Hay House books and products, or if you'd like to find out more about the Hay Foundation, please contact:

Hay House, Inc., P.O. Box 5100, Carlsbad, CA 92018-5100
(760) 431-7695 or (800) 654-5126
(760) 431-6948 (fax) or (800) 650-5115 (fax)
www.hayhouse.com® • www.hayfoundation.org

* * *

Published and distributed in Australia by: Hay House Australia Pty. Ltd., 18/36 Ralph St., Alexandria NSW 2015 • *Phone:* 612-9669-4299 *Fax:* 612-9669-4144 • www.hayhouse.com.au

Published and distributed in the United Kingdom by: Hay House UK, Ltd., Astley House, 33 Notting Hill Gate, London W11 3JQ *Phone:* 44-20-3675-2450 • *Fax:* 44-20-3675-2451 • www.hayhouse.co.uk

Published and distributed in the Republic of South Africa by: Hay House SA (Pty), Ltd., P.O. Box 990, Witkoppen 2068 info@hayhouse.co.za

Published in India by: Hay House Publishers India, Muskaan Complex, Plot No. 3, B-2, Vasant Kunj, New Delhi 110 070 *Phone:* 91-11-4176-1620 • *Fax:* 91-11-4176-1630 • www.hayhouse.co.in

Distributed in Canada by: Raincoast Books, 2440 Viking Way, Richmond, B.C. V6V 1N2 • *Phone:* 1-800-663-5714 *Fax:* 1-800-565-3770 • www.raincoast.com

* * *

<u>Take Your Soul on a Vacation</u>
Visit www.HealYourLife.com® to regroup, recharge, and reconnect with your own magnificence. Featuring blogs, mind-body-spirit news, and life-changing wisdom from Louise Hay and friends. Visit www.HealYourLife.com today!